CRISIS IN THE OIL PATCH

CRISIS IN THE OIL PATCH

HOW AMERICA'S ENERGY INDUSTRY IS BEING DESTROYED AND WHAT MUST BE DONE TO SAVE IT

DONALD PAUL HODEL AND ROBERT DEITZ

REGNERY PUBLISHING, INC.
WASHINGTON, D.C.

To Barbara Hodel and Sharon Deitz.
This book could not have been written without your invaluable,
caring, and intelligent assistance.

Donald Paul Hodel, Silverthorne, Colorado
Robert Deitz, Dallas, Texas
May 1993

Library of Congress Cataloging-in-Publication Data
Hodel, Donald Paul, 1935–
Crisis in the oil patch : how America's energy industry is being destroyed and
what must be done to save it / Donald P. Hodel and Robert Deitz.
p.   cm.
Includes bibliographical references and index.
ISBN 0-89526-502-8 (alk. paper)
1. Petroleum industry and trade—United States.   I. Deitz, Robert.   II. Title.
HD9565.H58   1993
333.8′232′0973—dc20   93-5882
                                                                              CIP

Published in the United States by
Regnery Publishing, Inc.
An Eagle Publishing, Inc. Company
422 First St., SE
Washington, DC 20003

Distributed to the trade by
National Book Network
4720-A Boston Way
Lanham, MD 20706

Printed on acid-free paper.

Manufactured in the United States of America.

10 9 8 7 6 5 4 3 2 1

Authors' Note

On December 9, 1993, as this book was going to press, the Clinton administration unveiled its plan to rescue the domestic oil and gas industry. The presidential statement was far distant from an attitude only months before, when the president proposed an energy tax that would have almost certainly destroyed the domestic oil and gas industry.

Even so, this latest initiative is inadequate. First, it proposes mostly to "study" ways of strengthening the domestic oil and gas industry; there are no promises of specific action. And, second, it does almost nothing to provide an immediate, strategically needed reduction of foreign oil imports and relief from the dangers of predatory foreign pricing practices that could destroy our domestic industry overnight. Instead, trust is placed on long-term solutions that cannot ease the looming threats posed by dependence on foreign sources for our nation's petroleum needs.

According to Energy Secretary Hazel R. O'Leary, the administration gave three reasons for the initiative announced on December 9. They were, according to Secretary O'Leary:

"First, it significantly augments our nation's economic well–being. Second, it contributes markedly to the comparative advantage our nation enjoys in the world marketplace. And, third, it enhances our national security. Without an economically viable domestic oil and gas industry, in the long term we will be much worse off." (Emphasis added.)

We could not agree more, as this book will make clear.

Secretary O'Leary also stated a fundamental fact about the economics of the domestic oil and gas industry. She said: "Letting these resources stay in the ground adds nothing to our country's income. We are no better off . . ." Recognition by the Clinton administration of this indisputable fact is crucial, and that recognition is extremely encouraging despite the structural flaws in the administration's proposals.

With this clearly understood, perhaps we can devise programs to avoid the disastrous consequences of decades of official hostility and indifference to the Oil Patch, which is the purpose of this book.

It is our emphatic hope that *Crisis in the Oil Patch* will provide some assistance and underpinning to the Clinton administration's initiative, and that it will contribute constructively to the debate over specific actions to be taken.

—DONALD PAUL HODEL AND ROBERT DEITZ
December 1993

CONTENTS

FOREWORD

From January 1981 to January 1989 I spent all my time in the Departments of Interior and Energy of the United States. It will always be a frustration to me that an administration supported by the American oil and gas industry could not do nearly enough in return. This is true especially because I believe that the energy industry forms the backbone of our economic system and our much envied way of life.

Many people did not know that the Department of Interior, where I was undersecretary and, later, secretary, has more to do with implementing energy policy than the Department of Energy. The Department of Energy, where I served as secretary for nearly two years, simply talked about energy policy; it recommended action, but had no power to dispose of energy issues. Interior, on the other hand, is charged with managing the one-third of the United States that is owned by the federal government, plus the Outer Continental Shelf where vast energy resources lie. The Interior Department has jurisdiction over the leasing, exploration, and development of truly huge potential energy supplies—not only oil and natural gas, but coal, geothermal, tar sands, oil shale, and other sources of power available to our energy-dependent modern civilization.

During my tenure in the Reagan administration, I came to know and respect many of the key players in the oil and gas industry. They were, almost without exception, dedicated patriots more interested in the nation's future than in their bank balances. These independent oil and gas producers were prepared to do whatever was required, within reason, to keep essential energy flowing to Americans.

And this despite the enormous hostility displayed toward "rich oil men" by politicians and many television commentators, some of whom take home more money each year for talking to us on television than many of those "rich oil men" they love to deride. So who was making the most investment in America? The oil producers who put their fortunes at risk, or the TV commentators who had more money available to reinvest in America than many of the people they were criticizing?

It's an interesting contradiction, but not one that will be explored in this book. Rather, it is our hope that this book will balance what most people read in newspapers and see and hear on television with a much more accurate picture of what is happening to the domestic oil and gas industry, why it is happening, and the consequences to all of us of these events.

—DONALD PAUL HODEL

It is an indictment of the nation's media that few business writers and editors at mainstream publications were aware of the depth of the difficulties of the U.S. oil and gas industry until the catastrophe was an accomplished fact.

The energy industry was an important part of the news coverage I directed and wrote about as executive business editor of and columnist for the late *Dallas Times Herald*.

The full impact of what was occurring in the industry in the first half of the 1980s didn't strike full force in most mass media newsrooms until the disaster was basically over. As early as 1981, certainly by 1982, it was clear to many people connected with the oil and gas industry that petroleum prices were starting to move into a sharp downturn trend, and that the consequences would be harmful, perhaps even ruinous to independent exploration and production companies. Energy industry executives were sounding the alarm. But most newspapers and newspaper editors—this one included—tended to look at the regional and local picture rather than the overall impact that declining oil prices, punishing tax laws, and increasing imports would have on the nation's security. That was our fault as journalists. We did not adequately educate people about the trend, or its grave consequences. For my part, this book is partly an effort to compensate for that serious error of journalistic omission.

—ROBERT DEITZ

So much has been written about the energy industry in the United States that it would be redundant to repeat most of it here. Instead, this book will be restricted to oil and gas and will not attempt to deal with such collateral topics as alternative energy supplies and the impact they have on national policy.

Such a self-imposed limitation might be called an incomplete effort, and in a broad sense that's true. But there's a good reason for restricting the topic. That reason is that the United States—indeed, the world—remains locked firmly into "The Hydrocarbon Age," as author Daniel Yergin so appropriately described it in his classic, panoramic history of oil, THE PRIZE: The Epic Quest for Oil, Money and Power.[1]

Ours is not yet a nuclear age, no matter how important nuclear power generation has become in some nations. Only France among the industrialized nations acquires most of its electric generation power, 72.7 percent in 1991, from nuclear sources.[2] According to the International Atomic Energy Agency, in 1991 the United States generated only 21.7 percent of its electric power from nuclear fuels, and there is little prospect that new nuclear plants will be built in the near future.

These numbers, of course, represent only generation of electric power; they do not touch on energy for vehicles, plastics manufacturing, and other widespread uses of hydrocarbons. Nuclear power is an important contributor to electric supply, but it will not displace fossil fuels as the primary source of electric generation in the United States or most other nations in the near future.

We expect that research and development will continue to exploit such potentially important alternative energy resources as nuclear (despite its limitations), solar, wind, and geothermal power, as well as methanol, oil-shale, and other sources of natural energy. Many of these may eventually come into play as hydrocarbon deposits are depleted or abandoned, which they almost certainly will be by a civilization that has come to rely on energy as a basis for everything from the most mundane of daily living routines (heating and lighting homes, electric can openers, home entertainment centers, transportation, and on and on) to the most visionary of dreams (space exploration, "thinking" computers, manufacturing robotics, to name just a few).

However important alternative sources eventually may be, our best estimate is that we will continue to meet our energy needs and with oil and gas for at least the remainder of this and the next generation of Americans, and very possibly several succeeding ones as well. Without some kind of energy breakthrough or aggressive government mandates, oil and gas appear certain to be our predominant fuels for the next forty to one hundred years. Oil and gas are abundant, cheaper to develop than most alternative fuels, and convenient (easily transportable); and they have a high energy-to-weight ratio, making them more economical than most other alternative fuels at the present time and for the near future.

Petroleum and natural gas represented 65.1 percent of all U.S. energy consumption in 1990, according to the Federal Energy Information Administration. That's down only 8.7 percentage points from thirty years earlier, and less than 7 percentage points from 1980. At this rate of change, less than 1 percentage point per year, it is statistically demonstrable that petroleum products and natural gas will continue to be our principal sources of energy fuel in the immediate years ahead.

If we are correct in this view, all standards of reasonable analysis demand that national policies encourage, rather than restrict, development of America's abundant hydrocarbon deposits. The stakes are high. Indeed, the issues involve nothing less than maintaining, or improving, the high standard of prosperity we have developed and shared with the world, and preserving our national security as the world's only remaining superpower.

That is why we have limited the topic of this book to the domestic oil and gas industry. Our purpose is to contribute to a discussion of that industry, its importance to our national survival, and the legacy we leave to succeeding generations of Americans. Finally, and most important of all, we hope to outline what can be done to save the industry—which has lost almost 500,000 jobs in the past decade alone and has the lowest rig count (or number of wells being drilled) since World War II—from the destructive course forced upon it by today's imprudent national policies.

It is our earnest hope that *Crisis in the Oil Patch* will contribute to the process of renewed debate on what can be done to salvage a vital activity that can still be described, without exaggeration, as America's most basic industry as we move toward the unknowns of the twenty-first century.

—DONALD PAUL HODEL AND ROBERT DEITZ

ACKNOWLEDGEMENTS ————————

Credit for this book must begin with millions of Americans who have put their lives and fortunes on the line to make this nation the most energetic in world history.

These are the independent entrepreneurs who have found the vast oil and gas resources that have made American life the envy of every nation on earth. America's independent oil and gas producers are among the nation's true modern pioneers.

Premier among them, for the purposes of this book, is Patrick F. Taylor of New Orleans, Louisiana. Pat Taylor is one of the last of the successful oil entrepreneurs to deserve the name "independent."

With no limited or general partners and no outside investors, by putting his own money at risk and believing in handshake bargains, in only two decades Pat Taylor has built Taylor Energy Co. into a successful oil and gas business with 1992 revenues of about $50 million. He has done so despite public policies that impede his efforts to create jobs, contribute to American economic growth, and reduce U.S. dependence on foreign energy producers.

Also, special thanks should go to Tim Woods, chief financial officer to Pat Taylor. Although a number-crunching bean-counter, Tim possesses an intellectual's view of the inconsistent public policies toward the U.S. oil and gas industry, and his ideas were helpful in shaping this book.

Other independent oil and gas entrepreneurs who willingly shared their experiences and contributed greatly to this book were Michel Halbouty of Houston and Robert Gunn of Wichita Falls, Texas.

Beyond these leading independent oil and gas producers and others in the industry too numerous to name here, several people have contributed much to making this topical book a reality. Begin with publisher Al Regnery of Regnery Gateway in Washington, D.C. It was he who believed the time was ripe for a renewed discussion of how this nation's tax and environmental policies were confounding reasonable efforts to avoid becoming wholly dependent upon foreign energy suppliers. Jennifer Reist of Regnery Gateway gently kept nudging the authors to keep the project on track, and Trish Bozell provided a keen editorial eye and helpful suggestions.

Add Don Hart of Hart Publications in Denver, Colorado, publisher of *Western Oil & Gas World* and other authoritative references that provided statistical data proving beyond any reasonable doubt that the "Oil Patch" where most of the nation's energy is produced is, indeed, in the midst of a crisis. Don Hart was also able to supply the authors with numerous contacts showing how the "Crisis in the Oil Patch" affects ordinary human beings.

The able assistants to Don Hodel during his tenure at the U.S. Departments of Interior and Energy from 1981 to 1989 are too numerous to list here, but Earl Gjelde, who served as chief operating officer at DOE and undersecretary of Interior with Hodel, deserves special mention for his valuable suggestions and advice.

Kent Simpson, a student at Baylor University in Waco, Texas, was a helpful researcher. Tim Phillips, a former worker for famed oilfield firefighter Red Adair of Houston, Texas, introduced us to geologists and others who provided valuable insight.

Finally, we'd like to thank Evan Fogleman of Dallas, Texas, a talented literary agent and skilled lawyer, who encouraged this project and helped it come to fruition.

We are indebted to all of you for your assistance.

—DONALD PAUL HODEL
—ROBERT DEITZ

CRISIS IN THE OIL PATCH

CHAPTER ONE

OCEANS OF OIL

AMERICA'S BOUNTIFUL SUPPLIES

Either faith in chance of near magical proportions or confidence in the awesome majesty of a Supreme Being is required to appreciate the abundant treasure of oil and gas that lies beneath the surface of the United States and its offshore waters.

Consider for a moment the natural process required to produce a single barrel of oil. It begins with plankton, the microscopic animal and plant organisms that anchor the ocean food chain.

Plankton are tenuous, often invisible, life forms that drift lazily or swim slowly along with the ocean currents. Some of them are arrayed by nature in spectacular neon colors and natural symmetrical shapes intended to attract mates or repel enemies. These attributes allow them to survive and flourish in numbers beyond human imagination.

Their abundance—the trillions of them—explains why these often microscopic organisms provide the basic sustenance for every other plant or animal in the ocean food chain. Plankton provide food for krill, salmon, and other human food and crustaceans, such as shrimp and lobsters, as well as mollusks in general. Even some subspecies of huge whales exist on nothing more than plankton, sweeping billions into their gaping maws each day as they graze the ocean's salt-water pastures.

Yet, over the millennia, enough of these plankton survive to die natural deaths and drift slowly to the ocean floor. Some geologists

3

estimate that the trillions upon trillions of plankton consumed by higher life forms in a single generation represent only about 10 percent of the plankton that ultimately die natural deaths and wash down to the depths. Even there some dissipation occurs before plankton are miraculously transformed into oil and gas. Countless plankton decompose before being covered with shifting silt. Even more of the lifeless forms that drift down become embedded in the ocean floor before decaying. And as the layers of silt above harden into rock, over millennia the heat generated by the increasing pressure and weight of surface sand, soil, and rock formations transform the remains of the dead plankton into oil or gas through a miracle of molecular change. This is stored as energy for mankind's use.

It is a never-ending process, one that continues today as evidenced by the oil that seeps naturally from the ocean floor in various places. To be sure, the plankton drifting to the ocean floor today cannot be used as energy for thousands of years. But it is happening.

Plankton are not the only source of oil and gas deposits. So, too, are the bodies of algae, bacteria, the planktonic crustaceans called krill, and on up the food chain to the herring, large fish, and whales that feed on krill. Millions of years ago, these organisms—not to mention all the other living flora and fauna that exist in abundance in oceans and large lakes—added to the stored energy that would ultimately become available. Every one of these once-living organisms helped create the huge pools of energy that lie beneath the earth's surface.

Today's hydrocarbon storehouses all began with plankton that lived as long as 300 million years ago, and as recently as only a few million years ago. These minute organisms provided the huge inventories of oil and gas that are now being drawn from beneath the earth, or awaiting the energy explorers' probing, diamond-studded drill bits. And it is here that the breathtaking scope of nature's hand in creating energy is fully revealed.

If it requires the remains of thousands of billions of plankton to produce a single barrel of oil, imagine how many of these organisms are needed to provide all of the nation's oil and gas deposits, plus those already discovered in the Middle East, Europe, Asia, and South and Central America. Evidence of the existence of large deposits can in fact be found on every continent, even Antarctica.

According to the U.S. Department of Energy's Energy Information Administration, through 1992 some 167 billion barrels of oil and 830.4 trillion cubic feet of natural gas have been drawn from beneath the United States. It all began when oil started flowing from a geological zone some 69 feet deep on August 27, 1859, at the first commercial oil well ever drilled in the United States near Titusville, Pennsylvania.

Like most other early oil discoveries, some of which can be traced to the earliest written history of mankind, the Titusville well was discovered visually. Oil was seeping from the ground. Geology was an infant science—petroleum geology did not exist at all. Early oil discoveries relied largely upon what an explorer for petroleum could sense, sniff, see, or touch. Thus, almost all of the early commercial oil wells of the nineteenth century came in at shallow depths of under one hundred feet, and many of these were near what are called buffalo wallows.

Buffalo wallows are shallow depressions in which roving herds of bison would roll their massive bodies in raw petroleum that had collected on the surface. The oil would rid the bison of and protect them from stinging insects and pesky parasites. As mankind advanced and bison retreated, buffalo wallows were covered by shifting soil and camouflaged by vegetation. But surface evidence of their existence persisted.

Even with today's sophisticated, computerized, seismic underground mapping systems and geological technology, the people who find oil still look for the lingering evidence of a buffalo wallow. A level piece of land with a slight depression that is not an ordinary valley, where treetops do not rise as high as the other indigenous flora, suggests that a buffalo wallow existed two, three, or four centuries ago. Other, more common, exterior indicators include oil seepages and porous rock formations that contain traces of hydrocarbon. These are the clues that early oil pioneers looked for before plunging drill bits into the earth, and geologists still look for them today.

That first well near Titusville set off a massive search for oil and gas in the United States. Petroleum explorers estimate that at the end of 1992—only 133 years distant from Titusville's 1859, not even the blink of an eye in geological time—the world's proven and probable oil reserves totaled slightly more than 1 trillion barrels. Only a fraction of that amount, 25.9 billion barrels, is in the United States.[1] This does not mean 25.9 billion barrels is all of the oil remaining beneath the soil and offshore waters of the United States; it represents only the proven reserves. Billions of barrels more are available, but they have not yet been proven through geological surveys. This is an important point, which will be dealt with in more detail later.

In 1992, the world consumed about 66 million barrels of oil each day—or about 24.1 *billion* barrels per year. The previous two years saw incalculable waste from wells set afire during the Gulf War or poured in the Arabian Gulf by Saddam Hussein.[2] The number of living organisms that were required to storehouse and provide energy on a scale this vast is incomprehensible.

But it is possible to gauge the wealth and power these energy resources have conferred upon the United States. Almost from the first moments of exploration of the North American continent there has been ample evidence of energy reserves. In the sixteenth century, Spanish conquistadors, scouting virgin territory along the Gulf of Mexico, used onshore surface oil slicks to caulk the crude boats they used to explore the energy-rich coasts of Texas and Louisiana. A century later, in the 1600s, oil slicks were logged off the California coast by mariners. (In centuries to come, these same oil seepages from the ocean floor would become ammunition for environmentalists who charged that oil producers "polluted" the environment). Eighteenth-century maps of England's middle American colonies, primarily Pennsylvania and Western Virginia, also noted deposits of seeping oil.

Even so, until the middle of the nineteenth century, oil was regarded as a curiosity at best, a nuisance to agriculture at worst. Farmers tending fields where oil had seeped had to plow, plant, and reap around the "diseased" soil. Some found it useful. Americans are a resourceful people, and snake-oil salesmen peddled raw petroleum as a miraculous curative power. Still others used it as a temporary lubricant. It was not until around the time of the Titusville discovery, however, that hustling entrepreneurs, assisted by expanding industrial technology and flourishing chemical engineering expertise, began to appreciate the real values of petroleum. And even this was limited to a single product—

kerosene—which was viewed as a potential replacement for increasingly expensive whale oil.

An inkling of the importance of oil to a growing population can be found in a classical piece of American literature. When Herman Melville published *Moby Dick* in 1850, he unconsciously recognized that the days of whale oil as a source of consumer and industrial energy were ending. The New England whaling industry was having to search farther and farther for the leviathan aquatic mammals whose rich stores of fat provided the oil that illuminated most of America's lamps and lubricated the spindles and gears of its growing industrial base.

Whales once were abundant in Atlantic waters. But, as Melville's Captain Ahab learned, by the 1840s it was necessary for New England's fleet of three hundred or more whaling vessels, the principal suppliers of whale oil, to sail to distant Pacific regions to find the large whale pods that made their harvest economical. The distance alone increasingly raised the price of whale oil. By 1850, whale oil was selling for about $2.50 a gallon to consumers (the equivalent of more than $20 in 1992 dollars).

The timing, therefore, of the first successful well drilled at Titusville in 1859 could not have been better for nineteenth-century consumers or, ultimately, twentieth-century industry. As raw petroleum was pumped from Titusville and other wells, chemists quickly adapted rude refineries to kerosene production. People were able to light their homes, offices, and power factories for as little as 10 cents or less per gallon. The rude refineries took crude petroleum and cracked it into millions of barrels of kerosene fuel that was eagerly bought by consumers and industry.

Three lusty new industries had been born—petroleum exploration, petroleum production, and petroleum refining. (Ironically, refiners at first believed gasoline had no real commercial value; it was too volatile for lamps or industrial burning purposes. The internal combustion engine changed all that.)

Over the succeeding years, American life and survival began to depend on oil and gas. The huge pools of oil and natural gas deposits found beneath the surface and offshore waters of the United States underpinned the nation's emergence as the world's foremost economic, political, and military power in the twentieth century.

It is not an overstatement to observe that this nation's global dominance in the twentieth century is directly attributable to the development of the enormous deposits of oil and gas in the United States. It was discovered in East Texas, and later in the Permian Basin of West Texas, offshore California, the Gulf of Mexico, beneath Alaska's North Slope, and in almost every state in the union in lesser quantities. Only sixteen of the fifty states do not produce oil and/or gas, although most of these have proven reserves.[3]

The profusion of U.S. oil and gas most often was discovered by wildcatters (those who drill wells in unproven territory) and usually developed by large integrated energy companies (companies that not only produce oil and gas but also refine and market petroleum products). It fueled the growth of huge manufacturing industries that provided conveniences on a scale never before known. Because of oil, we have propellants for cars and trucks, fuels for home heating, energy for water-borne steamship transportation, materials for industrial and consumer lubricants, feedstocks for plastics and agricultural fertilizers, gasoline and diesel oil for tractors to till fields for food, and energy for the machinery that preserves foodstuffs and for the trucks that transport food to markets.

Oil's influence on our daily lives cannot be overemphasized. If anything, it is understated. For example, in the federal government's monthly and bimonthly reports on changes in wholesale and consumer price changes, energy and food are not included in the definition of "core" inflationary trends. "Core" inflation, according to the federal government, consists of such items as housing, clothing, and even flatware and carpeting. But surely energy should be labeled the "core" of inflationary trends, because energy costs are, quite simply, a central basis for many, if not most, price changes for other goods.

In addition, oil has historical importance. Oil from Louisiana, Texas, Oklahoma, California, Colorado, and other energy-rich states stoked the engines of war that tamed aggression in two world wars. Over the years, the oil and gas industry has become as fundamental to the nation's social, political, economic, and military strength as our skilled and motivated population itself. Without oil and gas, the mechanisms of American commerce and industry, and especially its wheels of transportation dominated by the automobile, would quickly grate to a rasping halt.

Recognizing this makes it all the more distressing that the U.S. oil and gas industry and its major components—exploration, production, refining, marketing, and related activities, what we call the Oil Patch—have been thrust into crisis.

To put the matter succinctly:

The domestic oil and gas industry is being destroyed by imprudent public policies that are making the nation increasingly dependent on foreign energy suppliers. If current trends continue, within a few short years the U.S. oil and gas industry as we know it will be gone. And the nation will be relying on foreign suppliers—especially in the Middle East—for our modern energy needs.

The domestic oil and gas industry is being made uncompetitive and being driven out of business or forced to move overseas by a variety of public policies that severely restrict opportunities and penalize success. The independent oil and gas companies that form the backbone of exploration activities in the United States are being shut down, driven out of business. And the major companies that develop new oilfields, pump oil from existing fields, and refine and market petroleum products are being forced to move their operations overseas. *Fortune* magazine assessed the prospects of several major oil and gas companies in a 1991 chart titled, "Where the Big Ten Stand After A No-Growth Decade:"[4]

Mobil—"Major positions in the huge Hibernia field in Eastern Canada."

Chevron—"Focus on big-volume projects in Indonesia and Canada. Negotiating hard in the Soviet Union."

Arco—"Major undeveloped reserves in Alaska. Active overseas exploration program."

Phillips Petroleum—"Has been replacing [U.S.] reserves at low cost, exploring in Gabon, Somalia and New Guinea."

This massive flight of valuable capital and skilled labor from the United States can be directly traced to thoughtless public policies. In fact, it can be reasonably argued that these policies are forcing the withdrawal of valuable human and financial resources from the United States to foreign countries—the "expulsion of capital." These policies, federal as well as state, involve a complex mixture of punitive tax laws—taxes that discourage rather than inspire domestic exploration and production drilling—and restrictive environmental policies. The latter have been adopted in an effort to appease certain political pressure groups, especially those with radical agendas, rather than to promote ecological responsibility or the health and safety of the oil and gas industry and the public at large.

The result—a not-so-slow strangulation of the nation's most basic industry. The constriction is almost complete, and death will surely occur unless Americans develop new attitudes toward oil and gas exploration and production, and unless public policies change and encourage rather than destroy the industry.

It is a tribute to the tenacity of the people who work in the U.S. oil and gas industry that it has even survived in the face of official public ill-will and the hostility of many powerful segments of society. It is a testimony to the spirit of the men and women who, over the decades, have given their all for this vitally needed industry. These modern pioneers are characterized by a resolve sufficient to keep them exploring for oil and gas when seven to nine of every ten wells they drill come up dry.

The fact remains: Public policy today works to the detriment of the domestic oil and gas industry. That is why so many professional managers in the great oil and gas companies are increasingly moving their operations, investment dollars, and payrolls overseas. We are exporting jobs and importing oil, when we should be doing precisely the opposite—creating American jobs and reducing our imports. The economic and political consequences can be—and, unless fundamental changes in public policy are made, almost certainly will be—ruinous to our nation and our society.

Consider these statistics that illustrate the scope of the decline of the U.S. oil and gas industry:

Between 1980 and 1990, the number of people employed in domestic oil and gas extraction businesses declined by at least 30 percent, to 392,000 workers at the end of 1991 from 560,000

only a decade before.[5] This does not include the hundreds of thousands of additional jobs that have been lost because of plant shutdowns and the effect on jobs all over America due to the widespread uncertainty of energy price trends. (See Figure 1.1.)

Chevron Chairman and Chief Executive Officer Ken Derr has estimated that when you add all the collateral jobs that have been lost, direct employment in the oil and gas industry has dropped by more than 50 percent since 1980.

Compare this data with another industry—auto production. While the oil and gas industry was losing a huge chunk of jobs, many members of Congress lamented the decline of the auto industry due to

Figure 1.1
**OIL AND GAS INDUSTRY EMPLOYMENT
VS. OTHER SELECTED INDUSTRIES
1980 – 1991**
(Jobs in thousands)

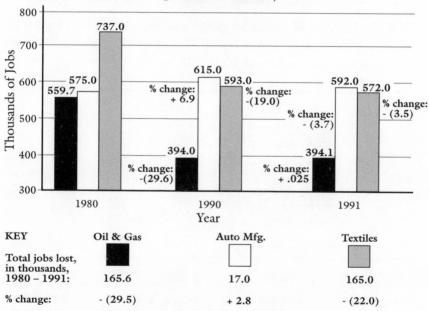

KEY

	Oil & Gas	Auto Mfg.	Textiles
Total jobs lost, in thousands, 1980 – 1991:	165.6	17.0	165.0
% change:	- (29.5)	+ 2.8	- (22.0)

SOURCE: Independent Petroleum Association of America, U.S. Bureau of Labor Statistics.

increasing competition from foreign automakers, especially the Japanese. Plant shutdowns in the Michigan "auto patch" got wide publicity. Members of Congress from states heavily dependent on the auto industry issued dark threats of trade wars to protect U.S. automakers.

Yet the number of workers employed on automobile production lines actually increased by almost 3 percent, to 592,000 in 1990 from 575,000 in 1980.[6] Other industries whose job losses have been widely publicized in recent years are textile manufacturing and steelmaking. Here is the comparison with oil:

If you take direct job losses in the oil patch and add the additional unemployment that has resulted from the decline in domestic oil and gas exploration, development, and production since 1980, *the oil and gas industry has seen its workforce decline by more than steelmaking, auto production, and textile manufacturing combined.*

To proceed with the statistical evidence of our domestic energy industry's decline.

In 1993, the United States began to import almost 50 percent of all the oil it consumed, up from 32.2 percent only eight years earlier. And worse, imports continue to grow. (See Figure 1.2.)

Industry analysts predict that unless the current trend is reversed, the United States will be importing more than 60 percent of all the oil it burns by the year 2000. And that is a conservative estimate; if recent trends were to continue, 75 percent of our oil would be imported by the year 2000. This is perhaps the most alarming of all statistical data, as you will see.

Between 1980 and 1990, our net dependence on foreign oil suppliers totaled almost 14.4 *billion* barrels. Today the United States is consuming about 17 million barrels of oil every twenty-four hours, and about 8 million of those come from foreign suppliers.

Almost half of our imports come from the politically volatile Middle East.

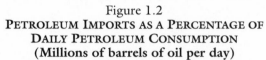

Figure 1.2
PETROLEUM IMPORTS AS A PERCENTAGE OF
DAILY PETROLEUM CONSUMPTION
(Millions of barrels of oil per day)

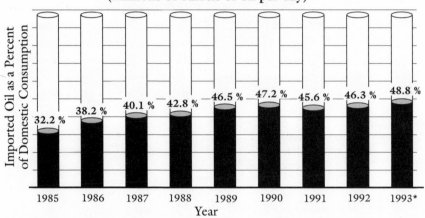

*For the six months ending June 30, 1993.
SOURCE: U.S. Department of Energy, Energy Information Administration.

"We are," says Charles DiBona, president of the American Petroleum Institute, "making ourselves vulnerable to a cutoff and increasing our dependence on a highly unstable part of the world." In July 1991, then-President George Bush warned that the nation's "energy future should never be at the mercy of foreign exporters." The warning has been ignored. We are already at the mercy of foreign oil producers, and certain to become more so unless we reverse policies to encourage greater domestic exploration and production.

Still more disturbing statistical data:

In 1980, the oil companies' share of total sales recorded by Fortune 500 companies was 31.6 percent; by 1990, it had dropped to 18.5 percent. The decline in net income recorded by the ten largest oil companies on the Fortune 500 list was similar, dropping from 36.4 percent of all Fortune 500 company profits in 1980 to 21.1 percent ten years later.[7] (See Figure 1.3.)

Oil companies have been accused of gouging consumers. It is politically popular to make that accusation. In contrast, it is not politically popular to point out that oil companies have been providing consumers with cheap energy for years, and the industry's financial performance reflects that truth. Over a long-term cyclical period of twenty years, the petroleum industry and all of its sectors—exploration and development, refining and marketing—have recorded profitability that is virtually the same as that of almost all other U.S. manufacturing

Figure 1.3
NET INCOME AS A PERCENTAGE OF STOCKHOLDERS EQUITY*
Oil Companies vs. Non-oil Manufacturing Companies
1985 – 1991

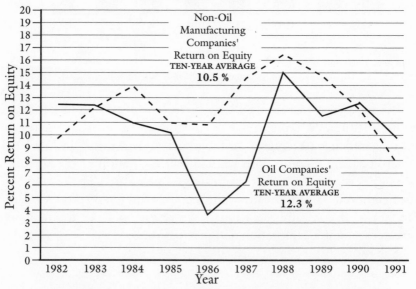

*Computed by dividing net income as a percentage of end-of-year stockholders' equity. The chart clearly shows that oil companies have earned almost 20 percent less on stockholders' investment than all other non-oil manufacturing companies in the 10-year period ending in 1991.
SOURCE: Standard & Poor's Compustat Data Base, as reported by the American Petroleum Institute.

industries. For example, between 1972 and 1991, the U.S. oil industry's return on sales averaged 13.25 percent per year (a basic indicator of financial profits, computed by dividing total profits by total sales). The average for all U.S. manufacturing industries was 13.22 percent per year, only 3/100ths of 1 percent less.

But disturbingly, the trend is now being distorted by the punishing tax laws and excessive regulations being put on domestic oil exploration and production. As a result, oil company shareholders are getting less for their investment dollars. For example, Fortune 500 crude-oil production companies' return on stockholders equity in 1987 was 7 percent, less than half the 14.4 percent recorded by all Fortune 500 businesses. Since the performance of oil companies was included in the average and thus lowered it, non-oil companies on the Fortune 500 list presumably had a higher rate of return on equity than 14.4 percent. By 1991, oil producers' return to shareholders had risen to 7.7 percent, but that was still below the 10.2 percent enjoyed by all other Fortune 500 companies at the low-water mark of a cyclical depression. (And, again, the non-oil companies presumably averaged more than 10.2 percent since the overall average was dragged down by the oil sector.) Since investors ordinarily put their money where they can achieve a high rate of return, a continued decline in return on investments in oil companies will ensure the drying up of capital the industry needs desperately in order to survive.

And yet more data:

A final statistic that cannot be overstressed is the number of independent oil and gas companies that have perished over the past ten years. Between 1982 and 1991, the number of independent well-drilling "operators of record" declined by 67 percent, to 4,244 in 1991 from 12,955 ten years earlier.[8]

This trend is alarming because the small independents have historically been the principal finders of oil and gas in the United States. They are the wildcatters, the risk-takers whose exploratory drilling rigs have discovered about 80 percent of all the recoverable reserves beneath the soil and offshore waters of the United States. As the domestic independent oil and gas producers become extinct, so does our national ability to find and pump the oil and gas American consumers require to satiate their voracious appetite for energy.

One critical aspect of the decline of the U.S. oil and gas industry is the human pain inflicted on the hundreds of thousands of American men and women who have lost their jobs in and out of the oil patch, and the hundreds of thousands more who almost certainly will become jobless unless we reverse the public policy that seeks to obtain cheap energy while making it economically impossible for a domestic industry to provide it.

The American public that demands cheap oil will eventually be forced to pay a stiff price. Presently, we have incredibly cheap energy. By anybody's yardstick, petroleum products are less expensive today than many other nonessential consumer commodities. For example, a gallon of unleaded gasoline cost an average of about $1.13 a gallon nationwide in December 1992, less than it cost in real dollars sixty years before. In contrast, a gallon of Coca-Cola cost about $2.20, a comparable measure of peanut butter $16, whole milk $2.50, and if you wish a dramatic comparison, a gallon of expensive perfume cost $35,840.

The point is this: Oil is one commodity that has actually gone down in real prices over the past few years, while most others have steadily increased by at least the rate of inflation as measured by the Consumer Price Index. (See Figures 1.4 and 1.5.)

Yet the major oil companies that dominate the retail market for gasoline and fuel oil have on occasion been accused of fixing prices and reaping windfall profits to gouge consumers who rely on gasoline.

If this were true, the major oil companies have been remarkably adept at botching the conspiracy. A gallon of gas in February 1991 cost you about $1.14 on average nationwide; sixty years earlier, in 1931, at the depth of the Great Depression, the inflation-adjusted price was $1.35 per gallon, *or almost 16 percent higher.*

Demanding cheap energy has grave implications. If it cannot be produced domestically, we will be forced to rely on cheap foreign oil. Therein lies the danger.

Figure 1.4
COMPARATIVE AVERAGE RETAIL GASOLINE PRICES, 1990
UNITED STATES VS. OTHER SELECTED INDUSTRIALIZED NATIONS
(U.S. dollars per gallon, excluding taxes)

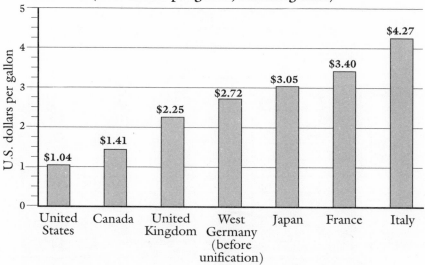

SOURCE: Energy Information Administration, U.S. Department of Energy.

Depending on foreign oil suppliers, particularly those in the politically skittish Middle East, poses a threat to our national security—and
it will intensify. The Gulf War was not an aberration. History has shown
that Saddam Hussein is not the first tyrant to try to put a chokehold on
the rest of the world. Trusting foreign suppliers for more than half our
oil invites blackmail by despots.

And the people who ultimately will suffer the most are not the
displaced rig operators, the geologists and seismologists, the tool
pushers, and other blue collar workers, but the entire American population, and especially those in the lower economic strata. Reliance on oil
imports means that foreign bankers, politicians, and petroprinces will
determine how much every American will pay to drive a vehicle, buy
food, heat and cool his or her home, and much more besides.

The consequences of continuing to squeeze the life out of the U.S.
oil and gas industry have such grave economic, social, and political

Figure 1.5
INFLATION ADJUSTED RETAIL GASOLINE PRICES VS.
CHANGES IN U.S. CONSUMER PRICE INDEX*
1940 – 1990
($ per gallon)

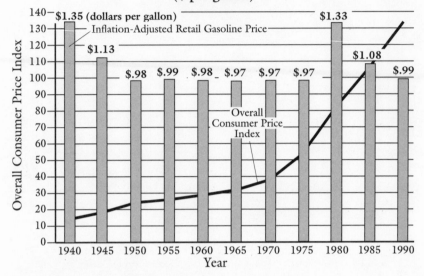

*CPI data indexed to 1982 – 84 = 100 %
SOURCES: Energy Information Administration, U.S. Department of Energy, and U.S. Department of Labor, Bureau of Labor Statistics.

implications, both nationally and internationally, that they can no longer be ignored. They not only imperil future generations of Americans, but our current economic, and, therefore, social and military strength.

The oil and gas trendsetters who provide this nation's energy supplies have been sounding the tocsin for years. Take Michel T. Halbouty, a highly regarded petroleum geologist and geophysicist and chairman and CEO of the Houston-based energy company that bears his name. As early as February 1987, Halbouty spoke about what punishing tax laws and unrealistic environmental restrictions were doing. In a speech to the Rotary Club of Houston on February 19, 1987, Halbouty said bluntly:

"When a nation's most vital industry falters, that nation begins to falter. In this regard, we have had [prior to 1980] a viable, highly productive petroleum industry. It helped to sustain our freedoms, but the government and the people lost the desire and passion to preserve it. So, as it dies, many of our freedoms die with it. The petroleum industry is at its cross-roads. Which way it goes, nobody knows, but I do believe that if it continues on the road it is now traveling, it will end in disaster, which, in turn, will be the beginning of the end of the United States position as a world superpower. We will then become a second-rate country—brought about by our own hands."[9]

The trend Halbouty decried in 1987 has continued unabated over the past six years. We are, indeed, venturing down a road that can and almost surely will dead end in disaster unless fundamental policy changes are made.

Solutions do exist. Remedies are available. They are not politically easy, but they are necessary if the United States is to continue its role of world political, economic, and military leadership and if it is to maintain a standard of living that is the envy of people everywhere. What we need are a clear understanding of the dynamics of the industry and the implications of its deterioration, and the political will to do what must be done to save it.

CHAPTER TWO

"DANCIN' THE PIPES"

THE OIL PATCH PARTY'S OVER

"I guess 'dancin' the pipes' was about the toughest job I had in thirty years in the oil patch. That's when I was working in an inspection yard. We had to roll those pieces of pipe—each one could weigh a thousand pounds or more—to get them in position [for inspection]. We'd do it by kicking them forward with one foot, balancing on the other foot. Four of us would work one pipe at a time. It was like lumberjacks rolling a log. We called it 'dancin' the pipes' because it looked almost like you were doing a forward jig on the pipe. It was dangerous, too. Slip and you could break or lose a leg in the snap of a finger."

—EEMAR "SONNY" LOWERY

Sonny Lowery is one of hundreds of thousands of casualties of the bust in the U.S. oil industry. At age forty-eight he lost his job in the oil patch when Horizon Oil and Gas Co. of Slick, Oklahoma, cut back operations in 1989. His seven-days-a-week job was to check the pumps of eighty-eight wells. He earned $250 a week, plus room and board.

Working in the oil patch was the only job Sonny Lowery had ever had. A

20

native of Tulquaha, Oklahoma, he dropped out of school at age sixteen to help his father make drilling mud and sell pipe. Like many oil-patch roustabouts, Sonny Lowery was a nomad. He worked for such major supply and service companies as McDermott International, and small independents like Horizon. He had been around the world—the North Sea fields, offshore Brazil and Mexico, Oklahoma, Louisiana, the Gulf of Mexico platforms off the U.S. coast, and the fields astride the immense energy deposits beneath the soil of East and West Texas.

In addition to dancing pipe, monitoring production, and making mud, Sonny had been a pipe inspector and an underwater pipeline installer, to name just a few of his skills. At one point in the early 1980s he was making $17 an hour. Some weeks he made more than $1,000, not bad for a high school dropout.

But then Sonny lost his job; employers were cutting back, shutting down production pumps, laying workers off. Not long afterwards, his wife and two children left him.

Today, Sonny Lowery lives in an abandoned refrigerator crate behind the Lipstick Topless Cabaret on Harry Hines Boulevard—"the street too tough to die," as it is locally known—in Dallas, Texas. He has become a street person. But Sonny Lowery's not a beggar. You won't see him on street corners, holding up a sign promising to work for food. He is too proud for that. Instead, he does whatever odd jobs he can find. Mostly he cleans parking lots for pocket money and eats when the Harry Hines bars offer free food to anybody who can nurse a beer for an hour or two.

In contrast to Sonny Lowery, Pat Nelson has fared much better after losing her job as a petroleum geologist in 1985. Now fifty-six years old and a divorced mother of two grown children she put through college—her daughter is a psychiatrist, her son a mechanical engineer—Pat Nelson has finally gotten back to the $44,000 annual salary she was making as a well-site and field-mapping geologist for the Gunn Oil Co. of Wichita Falls, Texas. (In purchasing power, of course, she would have to make almost $58,000 today to replace her 1985 salary.)

But she is not making it in the oil and gas industry. Her degree in petroleum geology has no application in selling eyeglass-frames to retail outlets. Pat Nelson is not bitter about the industry decline that cost her a lifetime profession, one that she hoped would move her into senior manage-ment with an independent producer. But she is nostalgic. "I miss the people," she says. "There's no finer group of people in the world than in the oil and gas industry. Their word is their bond. But I wouldn't go back to it, even if the industry improves and they started hiring again. Let's leave it to the young people. It's not possible to go back. But you can't just sit there for the rest of your life and say 'Poor me.'"

Begin with the Sonny Lowerys and Pat Nelsons of the nation if you wish to put a human face on measuring the decline of the domestic oil and gas industry. Impersonal statistics become more somber when they are translated into personal distress.

These are the stories of only two people who have experienced wrenching changes in their lives. Multiply them by hundreds of thou-sands, perhaps even millions, if you wish to understand the human distress caused by the industry's decline.

To get an idea of how sharp the drop has been, how many the people affected, look first at oil prices and employment. These are two of the fundamental measurements of the market dynamics of the U.S. energy industry.

After the oil embargo, led principally by Saudi Arabia and Kuwait in late 1973, the price of crude oil shot skyward. In 1972, the previous year, the average U.S. wellhead price of crude oil was $3.32 a barrel. By 1980, that figure had risen to $21.61, an increase of $18.29 per barrel, or *more than 550 percent.*[1] By comparison, during that same period, when high inflation was gnawing great chunks from people's salaries and savings, the Consumer Price Index (CPI) rose a relatively modest 97 percent—less than a fifth the increase in crude oil prices.

What is more, spiraling energy costs were responsible for much of the 97 percent leap in overall consumer prices between 1972 and 1980.

When you break the CPI down into its major components, you find that during this eight-year period, all energy costs rose an average of 15.9 percent per year; fuel oil skyrocketed by a devastating 23.5 per-cent per year, electricity costs rose an average of 10 percent per year, and pipeline gas prices almost 15 percent per year. Compare that with your basic food, clothing, and shelter price increases, which respectively were up an average of 9.5 percent, 9.8 percent, and 4.9 percent each year from 1972 to 1980.[2] Without spiraling energy prices, these certainly would have been much lower.

Nor was the upward corkscrew in energy prices over by 1980. In the next year, 1981, the average wellhead price for U.S. crude oil leaped another $10.15 a barrel,[3] almost 50 percent more in just one year on top of the 551 percent recorded in the prior eight years.

The response was phenomenal. By the early 1980s, the oil patch—a generic term for the huge fields of energy beneath Oklahoma, Texas, Louisiana, Colorado, Southern California, and Alaska, both onshore and off—became a whirlwind of frantic activity. Small independents scrambling to cash in on rapidly escalating prices sprouted like wild-flowers after a spring rain. They could not hire qualified, experienced people quickly enough to satisfy their search for oil. Roustabouts like Sonny Lowery were dancing the oil-patch pipeline jig with happy abandon and making better and better wages. Tool-pushers, mud-makers (people who fashion chemically treated mud that is injected into the hole to prevent or discourage blowouts and lubricate the drill bit), and pipe inspectors jammed airports to board helicopters headed for drilling platforms in the Gulf of Mexico, Alaska's North Slope, and off-shore Southern California.

Professional geologists like Pat Nelson were in constant demand in smaller, less developed fields. Landmen—oil and gas real estate buyers who negotiate exploration and production leases with property owners once potential energy deposits are suspected—were offered deal-cutting inducements that ranged from huge bonuses to company cars that they raced along back country roads to find property owners who could convey drilling rights. The land offices of both independents and major producers were doing . . . well, a land-office business.

Consulting firms offering geological and geophysical services prospered. The general aviation business soared to new heights in Texas, California, Oklahoma, Alaska, and Louisiana, as small airplanes were rented to make airborne geological surveys and helicopter fleets leased to provision remote drilling sites with men and materials.

According to the Bureau of Labor Statistics, 1.5 million people worked in oil and gas production in 1975. By 1982, the peak year for industry employment, the number had ballooned almost 125 percent to 1.9 million. But this number does not reveal the economic impact of oil-patch employment, because only 708,000 of them were involved in exploration and production. The remainder—about 1.2 million—were engaged in refining, transporting, or selling petroleum products.

By 1991, however, the ratio had gotten dramatically more out of kilter, with fewer than 400,000 people lookig for or producing oil and gas, while collateral employment in transportation, refining, and marketing totaled 1.1 million. (See Figure 2.1.) To get a better idea of how important the U.S. oil and gas industry had become to the domestic economy, we must backtrack to the exploration sector and then move forward to refining and marketing.

To explore for oil or gas, a geological team is needed—at least one person, the geologist, and probably a minimum of three. Once the geologist has found evidence that suggests oil and/or gas, you need a

Figure 2.1
U.S. OIL AND GAS EMPLOYMENT, 1980 – 1992
Exploration and Production Sector

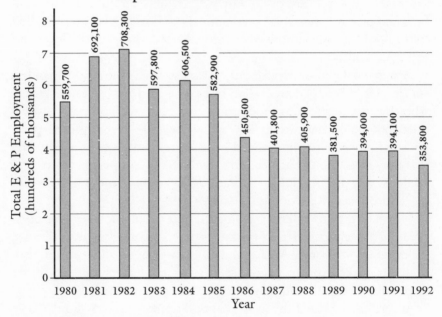

SOURCE: U.S. Department of Labor, Bureau of Labor Statistics.

landman to negotiate a lease with the owner. Then an exploration rig, say another fifteen workers. Thus far, a minimum of seventeen jobs has been created by one exploratory venture, and this does not include back-up office personnel required for record keeping, regulatory reporting, and other administrative tasks.

Assuming the well comes in, you will need a crew of at least four to prepare the well for production. The number could be as high as ten, depending upon the type of completion rig needed. Conservatively speaking, the number of workers is now twenty-one. This, of course, does not include the office personnel required for paperwork or the refinery laborers who transform the crude oil into unleaded gasoline, kerosene, heating oil, and scores of other products. Nor does it count the truck drivers who haul finished petroleum products to retail outlets, and so on. All of these people—at least another twenty-five for a total of forty-six, again by conservative estimates—owe their employment to a single exploration rig.

And this does not begin to include the collateral employment provided by businesses that supply the oil and gas industry with the products needed to explore and pump energy.

The steel industry is one example. It is essential for building rigs, fabricating pipe used to drill and case a well, and manufacturing the pipes used to ship oil and gas from wells to refineries or other processors and end users. One reason for a decline in employment in the steel industry in the 1980s was the collapse of the domestic oil and gas industry.

The effects of the collapse of supplier industries are exemplified by Lone Star, a small community in the piney woods of East Texas. In 1980, Lone Star was a bustling, thriving community of some two thousand people, a fourth of them employed by the Lone Star steel plant. The prosperity was shared by other nearby communities, such as Daingerfield, population three thousand in 1980, where small businesses ranging from barbershops to bookstores flourished.

But then, in the mid-1980s, as activity in the oil patch began to slow and drillers needed less piping and other steel products used to pump oil, Lone Star steel started to cut back production. The layoffs that began in a trickle became a torrent by 1988. Two years later, the Lone

Star steel plant could employ only a skeleton crew. The steel plant's parent company filed for bankruptcy.

By 1990, the population of Lone Star had fallen by 20 percent, from two thousand to 1,600 people in ten years. Daingerfield suffered similarly, with its population dropping to under 2,600 from three thousand. So had overall business activity in both communities. Many of the people looked for work in other cities. Strip-shopping centers that had bustled with activity in 1980 stood empty in 1990. The jobless rate of Morris County, in which Lone Star is the second-largest town, almost tripled to 16.2 percent in December 1992 from 5.7 percent at the height of the oil boom. By 1992, fewer than two hundred people were working at the floundering Lone Star steel plant.

While Lone Star may be an extreme example, it is not isolated. Many other areas not directly involved in oil and gas production have experienced similar depressions due to the breakdown of the oil industry. And steel is only one business activity that depends heavily on oil and gas drilling.

Others also are directly affected. One, as suggested earlier, is aviation service. In the early 1980s, helicopter repair facilities in Dallas, Houston, New Orleans, Denver, and Southern California started laying off workers; helicopters are essential in exploring and servicing wells, especially in off-shore fields.

Cement is another affected industry; cement is needed to transform an exploratory hole into a producing well. Oil-patch communities with cement manufacturing facilities, such as New Braunfels and Fort Worth, Texas, have seen significant job losses at cement manufacturing plants once wildcatters stopped pursuing oil and gas.

And none of this includes enterprises that stay alive by selling goods or services to the landmen, the geologists, the roustabouts and tool pushers, the oil company accounting clerks and truck drivers. Many landscapes around Houston, Denver, Tulsa, Lafayette (Louisiana), and Midland and Odessa (Texas) are littered with shells of buildings that once housed thriving fast-food restaurants, dry cleaners, banks, real estate offices, drug stores, and supermarkets.

In short, the intricate economic pattern anchored to a single exploration rig can have an economic impact far beyond the people that look for and produce oil and/or gas.

This leads to a second measure of the decline of the U.S. oil and gas industry—the exploration rig count. (See Figure 2.2.)

This weekly count, compiled by Baker Hughes Co. of Houston, is the basic measurement used by the industry to gauge oil-patch business activity. It reveals how many rigs are actively drilling for oil and gas and where drilling is being conducted.

Against a historical average of 1,828 rigs in operation in the United States between 1972 and 1979, the rig count soared to 3,970 in 1980—an increase of more than 117 percent. This alone meant almost 200,000 jobs, jobs directly related to exploration activity; perhaps five times that number were indirectly attributable to wildcatters seeking fortunes in the oil patch.[4]

When the oil boom collapsed, so did the rig count. Nor was it a gentle decline that allowed an accommodation from prosperity to poverty. Between 1982 and 1991, the average weekly count of rotary exploration rigs in operation fell from 3,970 to 862—a plunge of

Figure 2.2
AVERAGE WEEKLY U.S. RIG COUNT, 1980 – 1992

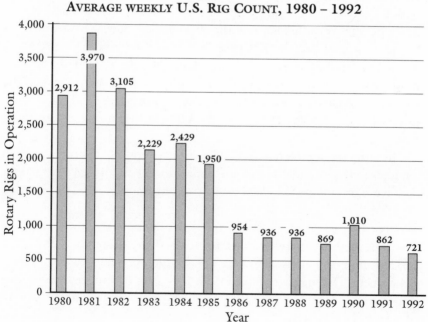

SOURCE: Baker Hughes Co., Houston.

almost 80 percent.[5] The effect on employment was devastating. In Colorado, for example, only about 12,000 workers were actively employed in oil and gas extraction in 1992, less than half the 28,500 earning paychecks in 1982.[6] Texas, Louisiana, and Oklahoma fared even worse, with oil-patch jobs in these three states alone falling by almost 55 percent, to a total of 244,400 in 1992 from 537,300 a decade earlier.[7]

Declines in production reflected the drop in exploration activity. In 1980, some 548,000 active U.S. wells, both onshore and offshore, produced a total of about 3.15 billion barrels of crude oil. By 1990, the number of producing wells had grown to 588,000, but they were pumping significantly less oil—only about 2.69 billion barrels—a decline in production of about 15 percent.

Several factors caused the steep drop in exploration of new sources of domestic oil, all of them related to reduced consumption and demand. One was a renewed emphasis on energy conservation. In an effort to assuage the proddings of Congress in the late 1970s, U.S. auto manufacturers hurriedly designed and built more fuel-efficient vehicles.

But Detroit was not just responding to congressional mandates. A more persuasive influence was the growing consumer preference for foreign autos, especially Japanese. For years, General Motors, Ford, and Chrysler had been producing vehicles that exceeded the new requirements for fuel economy. (These requirements are known as the Corporate Auto Fuel Efficiency, or CAFE, standards, and they establish gasoline usage guidelines automakers are required to meet under federal law.)

The impetus for Detroit to improve its products was not so much tougher federal standards as the competition from foreign automakers who were producing vehicles that many consumers seemed to regard as superior.

According to the U.S. Bureau of Economic Analysis, the value of domestic new car production rose to $104.7 billion in 1985 from $61.6 billion ten years earlier, or an average annual increase of about 5.4 percent. During that same period, U.S. sales of imported new autos leaped to $47.9 billion from $17.9 billion, or an average annual growth of almost 10.3 percent.[8]

But if government-mandated CAFE standards were a negligible factor, other federal efforts certainly reduced demand for oil consumption. President Jimmy Carter forced states receiving federal highway trust funds to lower speed limits on highways to 55 miles per hour on all federal highways, a move intended to reduce gasoline usage even though the law was widely ignored, especially in the West. (The limit on some highways was later changed to 65.) People were urged to turn off lights, and office building elevators bore signs asking occupants to "Walk Up One Floor, Down Two."

All of these were laudable goals, many of them promoted by federal policies. But the real impetus for reduced consumption came from the rise of energy prices at the consumer level. In 1980, for example, U.S. drivers used almost 6 percent less automotive fuel than in 1979. The decline continued for two more years. By 1990, fuel consumption for all cars, buses, and trucks in the United States totaled 72.4 billion gallons, only slightly more than in 1980, when 71.9 billion gallons were burned. This occurred despite an almost 21 percent increase in motor vehicle registrations, to 188.7 million in 1990 from 155.8 million ten years before.[9]

Consumer restraint in response to high pump prices did more to reduce demand than all the governmental pressure wielded in the late 1970s and early 1980s. In fact, the federal thermostat police became irrelevant and were quietly phased out of existence early in the first Reagan administration as consumers took over conservation measures. The result was predictable: The boom in the oil patch was over—oil prices began to slide.

Unfortunately for the U.S. oil and gas industry, energy conservation came at precisely the same time as the boom in drilling activity. When wellhead oil prices ratcheted up in the late 1970s and early 1980s, producers worldwide cranked up production to hitherto unknown levels. U.S. independents and majors spilled out into the oil patch to find new energy reserves and capitalize on the premium prices. They were joined by producers throughout the world. Between 1975 and 1979, OPEC oil production rose almost 14 percent, from 27.15 million barrels of crude oil a day to 30.92 million.

The non-OPEC nations boosted output from 26.19 million barrels to 31.76 million barrels a day—a 21 percent leap—during the same period.

Increased production, coupled with conservation measures, soon created a glut on the oil market. One contributing factor to oversupply was a decision early in the first Reagan administration to decontrol oil prices, which encouraged domestic producers to increase drilling and production activities.

And so, with the market awash in oil, prices began to fall, slowly in 1982 but accelerating steadily. From a peak average U.S. wellhead price of $31.77 a barrel in 1981, the average cost of a barrel of U.S. oil fell to $28.52 in 1982, $26.19 in 1983, and $25.88 in 1984. In the first quarter of 1985, it dropped to $24.12, and one year later to $18. By the third quarter of 1986, the average wellhead price of a barrel of U.S. oil had fallen to a low of $10.17 a barrel. In the years since, prices have recovered somewhat, hovering in the $20 range.[10]

Ordinarily, a per-barrel price of $20 would make it economical for U.S. independents to continue searching for oil. But two other factors came into play in the mid-1980s to cripple an industry already in trouble from oversupply. One was the growing pressure of environmentalists to restrict new drilling activities and impose costly regulations on existing operations.

The other was a tax reform act that penalized, among others, investments in petroleum exploration ventures. Subsequent chapters will deal with each of these topics in more detail. Suffice it to say here that by 1985, $20 a barrel was not a sufficient incentive to stimulate much new exploration in the United States.

Between 1987 and 1992, the average cost of finding a new barrel of oil in the U.S. rose to $6.88 from $4.31, an increase of almost 60 percent, while the average finding cost in the oil-rich regions of the Middle East and Southeast Asia rose only a penny, to $3.84 in 1992 from $3.83 five years earlier, an increase of less than three-tenths of 1 percent.[11] That might seem like a lot of built-in profit—the $13 differential between a market price of $20 a barrel and domestic finding cost of about $7 a barrel—sufficient to continue looking for oil domestically.

But the $7 represents just the cost of *finding* new oil. It does not include the even greater expenses of getting a well into production, transporting the energy to refineries, refining it, and getting it into the marketing pipeline. All of these activities are on top of the base finding cost of $6.88 a barrel, and they rapidly propel the production cost close to the $20 per barrel market price.

These were important considerations to producers when the price dropped to the $10 level in the spring of 1986. And that is because producers and investors were aware that such a precipitous price plunge could happen again, at any time, by accidental overproduction or deliberate predatory pricing practices by the OPEC cartel.

Even more significantly, the differential does not reflect the cost of replacing a barrel of oil drawn from the ground. This is a subtle issue, but it has profound tax implications that will be discussed later. The important point to keep in mind is that the finding cost of a barrel of oil is not the largest factor in determining the ultimate price consumers pay for it.

Because of rising finding costs and falling prices, along with other factors, most domestic production in the latter half of the 1980s came from older wells that had been found at costs well below $7 per barrel. Drilling expenditures for new U.S. wells dropped dramatically, to an industry-wide $10.9 billion in 1990, almost half of the $22.8 billion ten years earlier.[12]

What is more, explorers were being pinched by a lower drilling success rate. In 1980, drillers found oil an average of 30 percent of the time; by 1990, that had dropped to 23 percent. As if this were not bad enough, the productivity rate of existing wells was falling, from 15.9 barrels per day on average in 1980 to 12 barrels a day ten years later[13]—in sharp contrast to some Middle Eastern wells that flow as much as 10,000 barrels a day.

Quite simply, it had become uneconomical by the late 1980s for independents and major companies alike to drill for oil on U.S. territory unless it was a shallow field that did not require expensive deep drilling or a major field with reserves measured in billions of barrels. And none of these billion-barrel megafields, known as "elephants" in the industry, had been found on U.S. territory since the Prudhoe Bay discovery on Alaska's North Slope in the 1970s. This is not to say such fields do not exist. Ample evidence suggests they do. But for a variety of reasons, principally opposition from environmentalists, oil and gas exploration teams have been prevented from even looking for them.

We will discuss the impact of environmentalism more thoroughly in chapters 4, 5, and 9, but it must be touched on here in broad terms.

If every American were asked, "Are you an environmentalist?" the answer would be yes 90 percent of the time or more.

The environment is important to everybody. Nature sustains our human existence. No one wants to be cast as anti-environment, not even the most rugged logger, coal miner, or oil producer. But if you qualified the question, "Are you an environmentalist?" by stating that environmental regulations might add $2 a gallon to the cost of unleaded gasoline, that 90 percent figure would probably be substantially reduced. "Environmentalism" means different things to different people.

And herein lies the problem of defining "environmentalism": The environmental movement, as it exists, has come to be dominated by extremists who apparently prefer no development of any kind of natural resources, regardless of the harsh consequences a civilization, and especially the poorest people in a society, might suffer through no-growth policies. The movement is in desperate need of a more moderate and responsible posture, one that would balance environmental costs with economic benefits that accrue from developing these resources.

One reason radicals have assumed leadership of the environmental movement is because they have been exceptionally adept at manipulating the media for their own no-progress agendas. It is common to see television news clips or photographs in newspapers and magazines of suffering, oil-coated birds or seals, belly-up fish poisoned by toxic wastes, or forlorn owls perching on a single limb in a forest made barren by timber harvests.

But you seldom see the other side. This "other side" would be pictures of loggers, human beings, whose lives are literally endangered by steel spikes driven into legally cuttable trees by "environmentalists" trying to stop chain saws from whirring. And you seldom see any mainstream media accounts about the billions of dollars the oil and gas industry spends each year to sustain and improve the environment. Nor do you often read about the millions of dollars "environmental" lobbyists spend each year to influence Congress, the sweet perks their leaders enjoy from the small donations of tens of thousands of well-meaning Americans.

These activities do not lend themselves to sound bites, dramatic film clips, or still photography. Yet they are as real and as substantive as photographic images of damaged terrain and suffering wildlife.

A vocal minority in the environmental movement acquired political clout just as other influences converged to generate a genuine crisis in the oil patch. New and costly environmental regulations combined with reduced demand for oil, falling prices, and revisions in tax laws to put unprecedented financial pressures on all oil and gas companies, especially small independents with little available capital. Banks stopped lending money for oil and gas exploration, and started calling in notes when market prices began to drop.

On the heels of environmentalism and tax law changes, starting about 1985, energy companies began to plead bankruptcy. Many of the surviving U.S. companies shut down their domestic operations and moved overseas to find oil and gas. In one year alone, between 1988 and 1989, through exploration activities, 265 publicly held independent, major, and diversified U.S. oil companies added almost 100 million barrels of oil to their reserves. And every drop of it came from overseas exploration. Net domestic U.S. reserves dropped by 300,000 barrels in that year, indicating that newly discovered domestic oil or oil recalculated from existing reserves failed by 300,000 barrels to replace the oil pumped from domestic fields.[14] Total U.S. reserves dropped alongside.

In 1980, proved domestic reserves totaled 31.3 billion barrels of oil and 206.7 trillion cubic feet of natural gas. By 1990, these had fallen to 27.6 billion barrels of oil and 177.6 trillion cubic feet of natural gas, declines of 12 percent and 15 percent respectively.[15]

And this is just the beginning. Since 1988, the situation has worsened. The issue was placed in perspective by Charles DiBona, president of the American Petroleum Institute, in an August 1, 1992, article in *The Energy Daily*. DiBona's comments succinctly put the problem in focus. He wrote:

"U.S. oil companies have been forced to cut back on domestic spending and concentrate on investment overseas. Salomon Brothers' survey of 247 oil companies forecasts a drop this year [1992] of nearly 20 percent in exploration and production spending in North America. Yet spending by the same companies elsewhere is projected to rise by 9.5 percent.[16]

"Similarly, in the refining sector, regulations requiring expenditures that outweigh any possible gain have helped create a black hole into which American jobs are disappearing. Every dollar that we spend to alleviate a hypothetical or theoretical environmental risk involving emissions measured in parts per billion means dollars not available to fight real environmental problems or to create and protect industry jobs.

"Jobs are moving from San Francisco to Sumatra, from Dallas to Dharan. But the American people should understand that we are not abandoning the United States. We are, in effect, being thrown out. . . ."[17]

The obvious questions occur:

Why are we expelling a basic domestic industry? How could a nation be so shortsighted, so foolish, so unwise? After all, the dangers of relying too heavily on foreign energy sources are not new. They were apparent in the mid-1970s when Saudi Arabia and Kuwait turned off the oil tap, in the late 1970s when Iran used its oil in a power play, and again—even more dramatically—when Saddam Hussein invaded Kuwait in 1990.

These cases clearly illustrate the hazards of dependence when foreign suppliers use their oil reserves to influence internatonal politics and U.S. policies. A good example was the Saudi Arabia and Kuwaiti embargo of 1973 in response to U.S. assistance to Israel in the Yom Kippur War. Or the Iranian oil cutoff of 1978–79 after the shah was deposed and the ayatollahs wanted to punish the United States for having supported him. In both these cases, American consumers suffered inconveniences and higher gasoline prices.

To depend on foreign energy is potentially lethal, the equivalent of

playing Russian roulette with our strategic national energy requirements.

How did this come about? And why? What was behind the massive
dislocation of a basic industry over a ten-year period? And what can be
done to relieve the disaster? The search for answers begins with public
policies that have been more attuned to political exigencies and com-
promise than to rational considerations of our national prosperity and
security. Start with taxes.

CHAPTER THREE

"WHO'S KILLING THE GOLDEN GOOSE?"

A MYSTERY EASILY SOLVED, STARTING WITH TAXES

The opening sequence of the popular TV series, "Dallas," showed a pan-oramic view of pumpjacks—the bobbing, mulehead-shaped pumps that bring oil to the surface—drawing oil from beneath the Texas plains. The sequence was intended to suggest something about the wealth and power that accompany oil and gas deposits.

That view was of a field discovered by Robert Gunn on the Four Sixes Ranch in the Fort Worth Basin, in the north-central oilfields in Texas.

People in the oil and gas industry know Robert Gunn not for the "Dallas" introductory film clip, but as a widely respected independent oilman. He is a former president of the prestigious American Association of Petroleum Geologists and has been involved in the search for oil and gas since graduating from the University of Minnesota in 1949.

After college, Bob Gunn moved to Wichita Falls, Texas, and formed his own independent company. The location was good. Wichita Falls lies halfway between the rich energy fields of the Permian Basin in West Texas and the vast oil deposits beneath the piney woods of East Texas.

Though sitting on neither field, Wichita Falls is astride the less abundant but still profitable North Texas geological formations that contain energy deposits.

Over the years, Robert Gunn has been moderately successful in finding and producing domestic oil and gas. Or, at least, until the 1980s, when federal tax policies began to take a toll on his operations. "They [Congress and energy tax policies] cut off my legs," he says.

Gunn's problems—shared by thousands of other independent operators and the major oil companies—were initially due to a windfall profits tax imposed on domestic oil producers following the 1973 OPEC embargo. This tax was levied by an emotionally charged Congress in response to consumer anger that focused on high gasoline pump prices rather than on the real culprit—OPEC's oil embargo. The public felt falsely that oil companies were bumping prices of older, "cheaper" gasoline in order to gain unconscionably high profits from the crisis.

But this simplistic explanation, which was acted upon by a majority of the members of Congress, did not take into account the market dynamics of the petroleum industry. If you sell gasoline for $1 a gallon that cost you 50 cents, you don't make a profit if you have to replenish stocks of 50-cent gasoline with fuel that costs you $1 a gallon. Or at least you don't if you want to stay in business.

This seems like a simple explanation and one that could perhaps have been successfully argued, although without help from the media because the existing misconception would have been hard to overcome. It may be, too, that the oil and gas industry bears some blame for not having explained the situation adequately to the public and Congress. But petroleum industry leaders appear not to have been alert to the necessity of public relations until recently.

In any event, the windfall profits tax was just the beginning. It was accompanied by the virtual elimination of the depletion-allowance deduction which encouraged oil and gas producers to seek more hydrocarbon reserves. And the penalties did not end there. Of even greater consequence was a tax bill in 1982 which, although not intended to have a direct impact on the oil and gas industry, reduced the incentive to invest in oil and gas drilling ventures by almost a third. Until 1982, high-income investors putting money into a wildcat well could write off 70 percent of the investment if the well came in dry, spewing soil instead of oil. This *meant a top tax bracket investor risked only 30 cents of each exploratory dollar invested. But in 1982, the deduction was reduced to 50 cents, meaning that investors hazarded half of each $1 invested in a wildcat well. As a result, the investment funds independent producers relied upon to finance exploration ventures dried up.*

Even worse was on the way. The 1986 Tax Reform Act included what is known as the "Alternative Minimum Tax." The act eliminated any lingering tax advantages that might have stimulated domestic oil and gas exploration. As a result, starting in the early 1980s, Bob Gunn was forced to begin cutting back U.S. operations. He reduced the size of his company from fifty to twenty people. One of those he reluctantly let go was petroleum geologist Pat Nelson, described briefly in the preceding chapter.

Today, Bob Gunn is still looking for (and profitably finding) oil and gas. But the focus of that search has shifted from the United States to Africa, the Pacific Rim, and offshore China.

Begin with this simple proposition: The oil and gas business contributes more tax revenues, directly and indirectly, to all units of government than any other single industry.

But what about income taxes? What about sales taxes? Property taxes? All of the hidden taxes we pay, as individuals, consumers, and businesses?

The answer, quite simply, is that without the basic energy industry—oil and gas exploration, development, production, refining, and marketing—tax bills would be significantly higher. This is because the oil and gas industry produces huge revenues for all levels of government, and in their absence, the shortfall would have to come from other sources. And, as a result, America's standard of living would be much lower.

Yet today, the same industry that has made America's standard of living the envy of every nation in the world is being penalized by a harsh tax structure. And what makes this all the more curious is that energy lies at the bottom of the tax chain, just as the plankton that create oil and gas moor the ocean food chain. Energy is a golden goose being killed by taxation.

For many years, the U.S. oil and gas industry enjoyed a "depletion allowance" of 27.5 percent. That meant it could exclude 27.5 percent of all production revenues from federal income-tax calculations. The purpose of the law was to encourage oil and gas exploration by plowing funds freed by the depletion allowance back into exploratory drilling. But in the mid-1970s, in reaction to higher gasoline and home heating fuel prices, Congress virtually eliminated the depletion allowance on the grounds that oil and gas producers repaid the special advantage by gouging the helpless public. Nothing could have been farther from the truth, as the recent record attests.

In 1987, oil and gas companies paid $590 million in federal income taxes on exploration, development, and production operations, according to the Internal Revenue Service. Two years later, that number dropped to $505 million, or by about 14 percent. The reason was that during that period, total revenues—which produce the income upon which taxes are based—fell from $56.9 billion to $47.5 billion, a drop of almost 17 percent.

And why the decline in the federal tax take? Curiously enough, look at the taxes. Higher taxes depleted available financial resources. This forced energy companies to reduce production, which resulted in lower levels of revenue and income upon which taxes are based. In short, rather than wait for the goose to lay its precious eggs, Congress lopped off the goose's head in an effort to get the eggs before they were produced.

The oil and gas industry, moreover, pays a higher effective federal tax rate on its income than the average for all other industries, according to a General Accounting Office study of the 1987, 1988, and 1989 tax years. That study, published in August 1992, reported that the oil and gas industry paid an effective rate of 42.5 percent on net profits. This was about 10 percentage points—or almost 25 percent—more than the average for all other industries included in the study.

By increasing taxes on oil and gas production, Congress penalized major and independent oil companies and restrained them from finding and selling more energy. Production went down. As, of course, did revenues. Which meant lower actual profits and, hence, fewer tax dollars paid by producers. In short, by removing tax incentives and increasing tax rates on oil and gas, Congress actually reduced the Internal Revenue Service's total take from the oil and gas industry.

Similar results occurred with federal, state, and local severance and production taxes. For proof, look at the independent sector. In 1982, at the height of the boom in the oil patch, independent producers paid almost $7.5 billion in production and severance taxes on wellhead revenues of $135.7 billion, or about 5.5 percent of sales. Five years later, the tax take had increased to 7.4 percent of sales. But since revenues had declined to $72.3 billion, local and state governments took in less money—$5.3 billion, or about $2.2 billion below 1982.

The tax impact on downstream refining companies was even more severe. In the two-year period between 1987 and 1989, federal income taxes paid by petroleum refiners fell to $3.9 billion from $8.6 billion, a decline of almost 120 percent, according to IRS data. This was a result of higher taxes combined with falling profitability.

From these two areas—oil and gas production and refining—alone, the federal government lost almost *$5 billion* in revenues in just two years. And this was just the beginning. There was also the lost tax revenues from oil and gas industry workers whose jobs disappeared. The amount is impossible to calculate because of such imponderables as individual tax rates. But we do know that in the 1980s some 450,000 oil and gas production employees were thrown onto the unemployment lines. And since the average federal income tax paid by an individual filer was about $5,000 in 1989, this would suggest that the federal government's tax take might have been reduced by about $2.25 billion per year. Nor does this include unemployment benefits and welfare costs paid by taxpayers to the unemployed oilfield workers.

The impact of killing the golden goose ripples on, and the ripples become waves that wash most severely over consumers. And this for the simple reason that taxes on energy fall heaviest on consumers, regardless of the false information spread by "consumer advocates" and politicians who hope to win votes by attacking the "Big Oil" interests.

For example, in addition to federal income taxes, there are state-imposed severance and production taxes on oil and gas. ("Severance," because this kind of natural resource is thought of as "attached" to the earth; severance taxes have been as high as 30 percent of the value of the resource at the time of extraction, but are usually 10 to 15 percent.) These are passed along to consumers in all fifty states, although only twenty-seven states have such levies. Severance taxes in Texas, Colorado, Alaska, Louisiana, or California are felt by people living in Mississippi, Georgia, or Maryland because such direct taxes are paid in most cases by consumers, not businesses. (An exception would be natural gas consumers supplied by a utility that purchases its fuel through "hedged" contracts that require a fixed price. In such cases, increased taxes are usually absorbed by the gas producer, not the end user. This will be discussed in more detail later.)

Direct taxes are passed along to consumers throughout the economic process. When severance taxes are paid for a barrel of oil from Alaska, the cost is reflected in the price of tomatoes in Massachusetts. In 1991, severance and production taxes on oil and gas totaled more than $4.6 billion—all of which came out of the consumers' pockets.

As for the energy taxes the consumer pays every time the car is filled with gasoline:

- The federal levy runs about 18.9 cents per gallon. In 1990, before the 1993 tax bill adding 4.6 cents per gallon, a tax of 14.33 cents produced $13.1 billion from consumers.
- The states get their share—in fact, even more than the federal government. In 1990, state fuel taxes cost consumers an additional $19.4 billion nationwide. In that year, the excise taxes on gasoline in the thirty-two states that imposed such a levy ranged from a low of 4 cents per gallon in Florida to 21.9 cents per gallon in Nebraska. Since 1980, state tax revenues from vehicular fuels have risen exactly 100 percent, from $9.7 billion to $19.4 billion over the decade.
- Local governments have their hands out, too. In 1990, consumers paid $664 million in local motor vehicle fuel taxes.

  Added up, the grand total is about $38 billion in direct gasoline taxes. This sum, however, is multiplied because an energy tax is included in the "hidden" costs of other commodities we use and buy. When, for example, a retailer buys a product for $1, the product is marked up for sale to, let's say, $1.50. The extra 50 cents covers the retailer's cost of sales. And let's say that 10 percent of that 50 cents, or a nickel, goes to pay for energy costs (heat, light, transportation, and so on).

If energy taxes are increased by 10 percent, this means that we not only pay the cost of gasoline at the fuel pump, but we also pay a half-cent of the cost of goods bought at retail. This small percentage can add up to big bucks. Under this example, it means that if fuel taxes rise by 10 percent, a suit costing $199.99 at retail will be retagged to cost $209.99. The consumer pays the freight for high fuel taxes; it isn't borne by Exxon, Mobil, or 7-Eleven.

In addition to the direct levies that can be estimated, we pay fuel taxes based on gas utility bills; often, too, extra taxes are imposed on power produced by oil-fired electric generating plants. Energy taxes paid by consumer goods producers, processors, wholesalers, and retailers represent a portion of every dollar you spend for food, clothing, shelter, and all of the conveniences of modern life.

It is no exaggeration, therefore, to observe that energy is at the basis of many, if not most, other taxes we pay to finance government services. And yet government—primarily the federal government—has never really figured out a way equitably to tax the oil and gas industry.

By way of background, a brief history of federal oil and gas tax policies in the twentieth century is necessary here.

The development of the modern federal income tax system coincided with the infancy of the modern energy industry. In 1909, Congress approved an income tax on corporations, followed four years later by ratification of the Sixteenth Amendment to the Constitution allowing a federal income tax on both individuals and businesses. (An earlier income tax was levied to help finance the Civil War, but it was abandoned as soon as the conflict ended.)

The first controversies over how to tax oil and gas arose at this time. They arose because unlike most other businesses, the oil and gas industry derives the cash it needs to continue operating from the sale of its capital assets—the oil and gas deposits owned or leased—and not from the manufacture or sale of other materials.

This is not a minor consideration. For example, a retailing chain doesn't derive income from the sale of its stores. Neither does a steel-maker generate revenues by selling its furnaces or rolling mills. Ford and Chrysler sell cars, not assembly-line units.

And herein emerged the first knotty problem for lawmakers. The Sixteenth Amendment explicitly granted Congress the power "to lay and collect taxes on income from *whatever source derived . . .*" (emphasis added). But how could the sale of capital assets be taxed in a fashion that would have oil and gas producers pay their fair share, and still encourage them to continue finding more energy to replace the reserves they depleted by selling their only real capital assets?

The operative word was "depleted." For the first seventy years or so of this century, Congress and the courts hit upon a solution by recognizing that revenues generated by the sale of oil and gas were not exclusively "income" as defined by the Sixteenth Amendment and subsequent legislation. Rather, Congress and the courts determined that some of the cash generated by selling oil and gas was simply a recovery of the owner's capital investment. If that portion were not taxed, the owner's capital risk could remain unimpaired as the resources were depleted.

And so, for years Congress wrangled about how much to tax energy producers and what those taxes should be—especially during and after World War I when oil prices shot skyward along with the increased demand. Finally, in 1926, Congress hit upon the magic figure of 27.5 percent as a depletion allowance for oil and gas producers. In general, this meant that a producer did not have to pay income taxes on the first 27.5 cents of every dollar generated by the sale of oil and gas. (Granted, the depletion allowance contained other provisions that did not make this an all-encompassing rule. But it did apply in most cases. For the sake of simplicity, we'll not get into the minutiae of the tax code provisions for computing depletion allowances.)

Yet this tax-free "income" really wasn't "income." It was a return on investment, intended to serve as an incentive to seek new deposits of oil and gas. If Congress made a mistake here, it was in not insisting that the cash flow generated by the depletion allowance be put back into new exploratory ventures. That would have solved numerous problems the industry faced down the road, because many people erroneously believed oil producers were using the depletion allowance to live high lifestyles rather than pouring it back into the ground to find more energy.

Even so, until the early 1970s, the formula worked well. The depletion allowance encouraged U.S. oil and gas explorers to find more fuel to drive the expanding industrial base and thus serve the growing needs of a more mobile population. Even more important, the U.S oil and gas industry provided most of the energy required to fight a global war; throughout World War II, the United States supplied almost 50 percent of all petroleum products used by the Allied powers to defeat the Axis nations. Significantly, this was done at no increased cost to consumers (although, granted, it was accomplished through strict rationing and price controls).

Between 1925 and 1945, for example, the average wellhead price of a barrel of U.S. oil actually declined by almost 30 percent, to $1.22 per barrel at the end of World War II from $1.63 twenty years earlier. Consumer prices didn't fall so much, primarily because of the wartime need for fuel. Still, the pump price of a gallon of gasoline in 1945 was 10 percent below what it had been twenty years earlier, in both actual dollars and prices adjusted for inflation.

In consequence, substantial federal receipts were generated by taxing income on the 72.5 cents of every dollar raised by oil and gas production ($1 of production minus the 27.5 cents depletion allowance). At the same time, everyone from independent wildcatters to major oil companies used funds freed from taxation by the depletion allowance to search for more oil and gas.

Import levels also remained reasonable. Between 1950 and 1970, net imports as a percentage of total U.S. oil consumption increased sevenfold, but remained a modest 21.5 percent, meaning that the United States was supplying almost 80 percent of its petroleum energy needs. The wellhead cost of oil was kept at low levels, partially because of federal regulation and pressures to keep prices low. In fact, the wellhead price of a barrel of oil produced in the United States didn't rise above $3—about 7 cents per gallon of crude oil—until 1969, when the Vietnam War (and inflation) put strains on the overall economy as well as the energy industry. Between 1950 and 1970, for example, the wholesale price of crude oil sent to U.S. refiners rose only 26 percent, to 7.2 cents per gallon in 1970 from 5.7 cents twenty years before.[1] In contrast, the inflation rate (as measured by the Consumer Price Index) rose almost 62 percent.

Then, beginning in the late 1960s, two developments had a dramatic impact on the U.S. oil and gas industry. The first was the Tax Reform Act of 1969, the initial effort to position the neck of the golden goose of oil on the chopping block. As Frank M. Burke, Jr., chairman and CEO of Dallas-based Burke, Mayborn & Co. and an executive consultant to accounting firm Coopers & Lybrand, wrote in October 1992, "In hindsight, the Tax Reform Act [of] 1969 was the beginning of what became a series of devastating legislative and administrative changes in oil and gas taxation."[2]

These changes were complex measures that, basically, reduced the percentage depletion rate for oil and gas production from 27.5 to 22 percent. This effectively reduced the amount of cash available for exploration and production drilling by more than 5 percent of gross revenues. But the tax reformers weren't through. In addition, the 1969 law increased taxes on production if the percentage depletion was higher than the actual cost of pumping oil and gas from beneath the ground. If, that is, the depletion allowance was 22 cents per dollar, but the actual cost of drilling for new oil was 15 cents per dollar, you did not get the higher amount as a tax deduction. Instead, you paid taxes on the 7 cent differential between the depletion allowance and your actual cost.

This had a severe effect on the people who find oil and gas. As consultant Frank Burke observed, "While no tangible evidence exists to confirm the fact, many industry observers believe that the reduction in the percentage depletion rate was directly responsible for a significant part of the decline of approximately 20 percent in the number of wells completed in the U.S. between 1969 [the last year of the 27.5 percent depletion rate] and 1971."[3]

But even the 1969 Act wouldn't have been crushing if it had not been followed a few short years later by the second, far more important development: the creation of the Organization of Petroleum Exporting Countries in the early 1970s.

With the creation of OPEC, an oil-rich, thirteen-nation cartel of Third World nations dominated by Arabian Gulf countries, the equilibrium of the world petroleum industry—perhaps the political structure of the world—was forever altered. From that moment on, petroleum became a commodity that could influence and shape the international geopolitical structure. The OPEC nations controlled almost 75 percent of the world's 532.5 billion barrels of proven crude-oil reserves in 1970.[4] More importantly, at least half of these reserves were in countries run by fundamentalist Moslem or revolutionary Arab governments which were bitterly hostile to Israel and its allies. With the arrival of OPEC, oil became a weapon of diplomacy as well as war. The Arabian Gulf nations did not delay in wielding the arsenal of energy that lay beneath their shifting desert sands.

The Yom Kippur War of 1973 and the OPEC oil embargo that retaliated against U.S. aid to Israel is history. The significance here is that the joint Egyptian-Syrian assault on Israel was not so much a military effort to destroy an enemy as a political mission to drive home to Western oil-consuming nations—primarily, the United States—the growing petropolitical power of Arabian Gulf nations. The point was well made.

The Saudi- and Kuwaiti-led embargo created gasoline shortages in the United States. Millions of Americans were inconvenienced—not hurt, but inconvenienced—by lengthy lines of autos awaiting the short and increasingly more expensive gasoline supplies. It ought to have taught U.S. consumers that fuel was not to be taken for granted. But U.S. consumers, and their representatives in Congress, missed the point because of an incongruous and politically inappropriate occurrence.

Instead of faulting the OPEC nations for withholding supplies, U.S. consumers and politicians blamed the oil crisis on the major oil companies that provided most of the fuel used for transportation, home-heating, and industrial purposes. They failed to understand that North America was no longer the service station for the globe.

Before OPEC, the major oil companies—the "Seven Sisters"—set market prices by controlling supplies to fit demand. But afterwards, almost overnight, U.S. reserves seemed unnecessary as cheap fuel imports began to rise. From then on, the market would be dominated by Middle Eastern petroprinces, not the Seven Sisters. As James L. Dunlap, president of Texaco, remarked in a speech to the Forum Club of Houston in October 1991: "The oil shocks of the 1970s reminded us with brutal forcefulness how much we need oil, and how great a force the Middle East [is] . . . in its production."[5]

As primary spokesman for one of the Seven Sisters, Dunlap understated the problem. After OPEC, oil prices were no longer determined by the U.S. industry and its customers but by the Middle East producers.

Facts notwithstanding, some members of Congress and public consumer advocates began to blame major U.S. and independent oil companies for the doubling of oil prices following the 1973 OPEC embargo. Congressional hearings included a parade of bewildered major oil-company executives, who believed they were being treated like so many Nazi war criminals.

Their principal accuser was Democratic Senator Henry (Scoop) Jackson of Washington, chairman of the Senate committee that conducted the inquiry into rising oil prices. Jackson, ordinarily a remarkably reasonable statesman and responsible man who had sought to balance environmental concerns with rational economic considerations, he all but condemned the oil company CEOs to the gallows in response to consumer anger over scarce fuel for autos and rising prices for home heating oil in the northeastern United States. Jackson cannot be wholly blamed, having scented the powerful aroma of the White House. In a democracy, political ambitions can explain a multitude of actions. Of equal importance was the seeming arrogance of the oil industry toward consumer public relations, quite unlike Congress's acute sensitivity to it.

Public relations is not a small matter. But oil and gas producers historically have been insensitive to it, and for several possible reasons. One is that wildcatters are fiercely independent people who don't like to ask permission for anything from anyone. Another is that the oil industry can be an immensely powerful source of political money. Why scatter funds to buy (or maybe not buy) public good will when you can target those funds to support key friendly politicians who share your views? Consumers must have fuel, and politicians must have campaign contributions. Politically, the argument makes sense.

Whatever the reasons, not until after the congressional hearings of the mid-1970s did the oil industry realize the importance of positive as well as defensive public relations and start to act accordingly.

On Capitol Hill, some members of Congress, as usual, were playing to the crowd. They were running with the hare and hunting with the hounds, trying to have it both ways and succeeding. Members of Congress and others with any knowledge at all of the oil and gas business knew that U.S. oil and gas producers had nothing to do with the sharp rise in consumer fuel prices in 1973. If matters had been left to domestic producers, consumer prices would certainly not have risen.

The statistically demonstrable fact is that the U.S. oil and gas industry, both then and now, has done no better, and largely worse, in terms of profitability than most other major domestic industries. Like most other industries, the U.S. oil and gas business has cyclical profits. And over the long haul, it has tracked the same general profit patterns as most other domestic industries.

But facts can confuse politics. And so, because U.S. oil and gas companies continued to make profits and pay dividends during the OPEC embargo crisis, they were penalized by politicians who were seeking populist favor rather than facing the Arab embargo in terms of what it meant for the nation then and what it could mean in the years ahead.

The result was that in 1980, after a second price and shortage shock imposed by Iran's oil embargo, Congress approved a tax that penalized what it called "windfall profits" enjoyed by the oil and gas industry. Nor did Congress stop there. In addition, the populist reformers effectively began to roll back the depletion allowance that encouraged new oil and gas exploration. Having already been reduced by the 1969 Tax Reform Act to 22 percent from 27.5 percent, Congress now cut it back to 15 percent—and allowed it for only the first 5,000 barrels per day pumped by domestic companies. This effectively eliminated the depletion allowance for major oil companies, which drew much more oil than that from the ground daily. The windfall profits tax applied to the independents as well.

As a result of these two measures, it became vastly more difficult for oil and gas producers to continue looking for new domestic energy supplies, especially after the price of oil peaked at almost $40 a barrel in the 1979–81 period.

Robert Gunn, the independent oil and gas producer touched on briefly, is a good illustration of a hard-put oil and gas producer.

In 1981, the average wellhead price for U.S. oil was about $32, down from the heady $40 level of a year or two earlier. That certainly seemed enough to guarantee a search for new oil to replace what was being pumped from the ground and shipped to refiners. After all, finding costs for previously discovered oil were running only about $8–$10 per barrel in 1981. The difference between $32 and $8–$10 is $22–$24 per barrel. Windfall profits? On the surface, it would certainly seem so. But take a brief look at what Robert Gunn actually made from that $32 per barrel of oil.

Begin with the state severance tax of $1.47. Then subtract the windfall profits tax of $14.70. Then the cost of about $6.83 for production rigs to lift the oil from its underground bedrest. Total: $24. That makes a profit of roughly $4.50 per barrel as an incentive for Robert Gunn to look for new domestic oil and gas reserves.

And still to come are the federal income taxes of 50 percent on pre-tax profits. So take away $2.25. This leaves Gunn Oil Co. with a total of $2.25 per 42-gallon barrel to continue looking for oil that at that time cost him about $8 to $10 per barrel to find. Which means that he would lose $7 on every barrel of U.S. oil (or its natural gas equivalent) that he discovered. And this doesn't even include the ravages of discounting Gunn's future income stream back to the present.

So Gunn looked overseas and saw a much brighter profit picture. If he were going to risk the same money, he would do so where the rate of return was much better. That's what capitalism is all about.

Which, of course, meant that Robert Gunn would be extremely more selective in looking for energy deposits in the United States and its territories. Which further meant that thirty people, including Pat Nelson, lost their jobs. The jobs didn't vanish because Robert Gunn wanted to put people out of work to cut expenses and reap "windfall" profits. The jobs disappeared because the new tax policies penalized oil and gas producers—and other innocent people as well.

The windfall profits tax was, in fact, a windfall for the government, however disastrous for the oil and gas producers. But it was only a temporary windfall and not so great as the tax experts predicted. In the eight years between 1980 and 1988, the year the windfall profits provision finally was removed from the statutes, the tax yielded an additional $88 billion in tax revenues to the Treasury, fully $50 billion less than the $138 billion tax writers estimated it would raise in the decade.[6] More importantly, though, this $88 billion "windfall tax" the industry paid could have created additional jobs through increased productivity. The inescapable fact is that squeezing this amount of money from an already capital-short domestic industry intensified a problem that was growing worse almost daily.

Another reason for the loss of jobs was the Tax Reform Act of 1986. This law had the admirable intent of simplifying the tax code. But in the attempt, it all but destroyed inducements for investing in wildcatting for oil and gas.

Earlier rising prices for oil had given more affluent people an incentive to invest excess cash in oil and gas exploration. So had tax laws by allowing significant write-offs for investments that might not pay off.

This was not a special favor. Remember, the success ratio for wildcat drilling is roughly 10 percent, sometimes 20 percent; or, if you are really lucky, 30 percent of the wells. If you were in a top tax bracket of 70 percent, winning only two or three times for every ten throws of the dice would be a loss that would be financed partially through tax advantages with people investing "30-cent dollars."

But when, in 1982, the 70 percent figure was reduced to 50 percent, these investors would be speculating with 50-cent dollars, not 30-cent dollars. It was too much for all but the most speculative investors, and capital for oil and gas exploration began to dry up. Then the 1986 Tax Reform Act removed even these incentives, and new investment dollars for petroleum exploration vanished almost overnight.

Critics of the oil and gas industry would have you believe that the problem was strictly one of falling oil and gas prices. But that situation was exacerbated by higher taxes. How can you spend money to find more oil if (1) you are receiving less money when you sell your product; (2) your taxes are rising on the product you are selling; and (3) changes in federal tax laws are drying up your ability to raise capital for new projects? The answer: you can't, so you cut back your operations. And unemployment climbs.

Even so, Congress wasn't through with the industry. The reasoning seemed to be that the government could wrench as much tax revenue from a declining industry as it could from a healthy one. As *Fortune* magazine reported on March 3, 1986, "Congress is as excited about the oil price slide as a wildcatter watching a gusher. Members searching for revenue to cut the deficit or finance tax-rate reductions see cheaper oil as a painless way to get it."

And so, in addition to eliminating incentives, Congress came up with a new, even more abusive measure. In the 1986 Tax Reform Act, Congress adopted what it called an "alternative minimum tax." Essentially, it was a separate federal income tax system with different rules about how a taxpayer could deduct certain expenses, and how those expenses could be paid for tax purposes. The "alternative minimum tax" is an extremely complex code that applies to all corporate and many individual taxpayers. The impact on the energy industry was to tighten restrictions on the benefits provided to the oil and gas industry for exploration. In this respect, the new AMT axe fell more sharply on the oil and gas industry than on most other businesses, except, perhaps, real estate.

At bottom, what the alternative minimum tax did was to make oil and gas producers pay taxes on certain non-cash benefits, while excluding other cash deductions. In some cases, the AMT forced drillers to fork over taxes even if they weren't generating enough cash to pay them. This sharply reduced the amount of cash available to finance drilling for new energy deposits. Worse, the AMT discouraged outside investors from putting cash into oil and gas drilling partnerships, thus drying up another source of capital.

And so, from 1986 on, the industry went into a tailspin. The cumulative effects of reducing the depletion allowance, adding a windfall profits tax, removing investment incentives, and imposing an alternative minimum tax meant less exploratory activity in the United States and its possessions. This, in turn, meant fewer jobs and declining tax revenues to all levels of government. The tax police were gutting the goose to get at the golden eggs before they could be laid.

No wonder that during the 1985–1990 period domestic oil production fell almost 19 percent, to 7.3 million barrels per day in 1990 from 9 million daily barrels only six years earlier. Or that imports rose to 5.9 million barrels a day in 1990 from 3.2 million barrels a day in 1985—an increase of more than 80 percent. Or that the total number of wells drilled dropped a breathtaking 57 percent, to 28,513 from 67,821, during the same period. Or that the oil and gas industry's contribution to the U.S. Gross National Product fell from $114.1 billion to $95.6 billion from 1985 to 1990.

But the horror story continues. Government policies, primarily federal, are making the United States even more dependent on foreign oil suppliers like Saddam Hussein, Kuwaiti sheiks, Saudi princes, and Iranian imams.

Taxes are only part of the tale. To get a more complete picture, you also must look at federal "environmental" and "health and safety" regulations. Not everything labeled "environmental" relates to the environment, and not all of the regulations under the heading "health and safety" have any significant relationship to those topics.

It has become politically correct to support anything, no matter how insane, if it purports to aid the "environment" or "health and safety" generally. The very fact that these are politically favored topics ought to spur people to look closely at the claimed benefits. Common sense tells us that all kinds of interests will rally under a popular banner and seek to appropriate the popular label in order to gain economic or political advantage. And this is true regardless of the legitimacy of the label. Careful scrutiny is required by thoughtful observers in such circumstances, even though it guarantees that the political thought police will dub the observer as being anti-environment or anti-health and safety.

DONALD PAUL HODEL:
I'm reminded of this problem in a different setting. On one occasion, I questioned an item in a local school budget and was promptly labeled

"anti-education." On a more exalted level, the energy minister of an OPEC nation, who also ran the state oil and gas company, told me that he was accused of "undermining the revolution" when he cut seventy thousand employees from the energy operation. He replied, "No, if I wanted to undermine the revolution I would have retained the seventy thousand employees" (thus bankrupting the state-run company).

The point here is that cynical people with a self-serving agenda will always wrap themselves in self-righteousness to further their objectives. Healthy skepticism is an appropriate response to such claims and labels. This has special meaning for people trying to interpret what some so-called "environmentalists" say about the oil and gas industry.

CHAPTER FOUR

THE GOLDEN GOOSE MURDER

WHAT'S A BIG-HORN SHEEP WORTH— $200 OR $50 MILLION?

The Western big-horn sheep is a magnificent animal. It can weigh 250 pounds or more, and dances gracefully from rock to rock, defying gravity. Its sense of balance would be the envy of a ballet dancer or Olympic gymnast. The Western big-horn sheep leaps about mountain slopes, grazing on sparse vegetation and following the hillside flora lines as they recede in winter and advance in summer. During mating season, the rams compete for the ewes' attention by butting huge horns with a clashing power that has inspired musicians and football defensive linemen alike. That the big-horn sheep has accomplished all of this on small cloven hooves is even more of a miracle than that it has provided promotional visuals for the politically oriented television show "Crossfire." How, then, do you put a value on this majestic beast? And, were it possible, what would that value be?

To Utah environmental extremists, the value seems to be at least $50 million per head. And that is because these extremists prevented the drilling of $500 million worth of oil to "protect" ten big-horn sheep—

even though the sheep didn't live in a protected area and weren't threat-
ened by the drilling. Subsequently, the state of Utah issued hunting
licenses to stalk and kill the majestic beasts because state wildlife experts
deemed them more than plentiful.

Meanwhile, 25 million barrels of oil lay untouched. National depen-
dence on foreign suppliers continued. Numerous jobs were not created.
The Moab, Utah, area lost significant potential tax revenues. And the
nation's trade deficit increased by up to $500 million over a period
of years.

All of this occurred because a handful of environmental extremists
either ignored or simply did not care about the true cost of their opposition
to drilling for oil.

But were the environmentalists really concerned about the ten big-horn
sheep? Or was their opposition merely a mindless antidrilling sentiment
that substitutes capricious emotionalism for thoughtful analysis? A strong
case can be made for the latter argument, because the incident makes no
sense. Indeed, a costly peculiarity of the environmental movement is that
cost-benefit considerations are eschewed in favor of politically correct
arguments. But more on this later.

The early stages of many human activities throughout history have, by
today's standards, been everything from crude to ugly.

Take medicine, especially surgery. Until after the American Civil
War, surgeons were more butchers and/or barbers than healers. Lack-
ing modern anesthetics, the surgeons used alcohol to numb patients,
and leeches were used to draw blood and bring the bodily fluids of the
patients back into balance. As for food processing, the Chicago
slaughterhouses, where most of the nation's processed beef was produced in the nineteenth century, were such shocking places that they
inspired the lurid journalism that earned the once honorable but since
discredited title of "muckraker." Not to mention sewage and waste
disposal in cities. Or the treatment of laborers, especially children, in
the early years of the Industrial Revolution.

The point is: today's modern industries are judged by the sins of
yesterday. Granted, the early activities of America's mineral, mining,
and other industries were not environmentally pretty. But coal mining,

logging, and oil and gas drilling differ only in their particulars from excesses committed in other areas before the advance of technology and the development of corporate social consciousness.

For the past three decades, however, America's extractive industries have generally responded responsibly to public demands for environmentally sound use of the earth's resources. People hostile to all extractive industries dispute this, of course. But an objective, rational examination of the facts demonstrates otherwise. A glance at the background.

America has always had its environmentalists. But until recently they have not been called that. Until the early 1950s, they were more often known as naturalists—nature artist John J. Audubon, explorer John Muir, park designer Frederick Law Olmstead, and President Theodore Roosevelt leap to mind. By and large, the "naturalists" did little more than impress others with the beauty of nature through their paintings, photographs, and words. A major exception to this rule in the late nineteenth and early twentieth centuries was the establishment and expansion of our national parks system, much of it attributable to Theodore Roosevelt. Even so, until modern times, extractive industries had few barriers to prevent them from carelessly exploiting America's copious natural resources.

In the 1800s, for example, as civilization advanced from the Eastern seaboard toward the Pacific Ocean, loggers cut away millions of acres of timber to build houses, bridges, canals, and more for the growing population, but without giving much thought to replacing the precious wood. This was especially true in the western part of the country, where noble ranks of redwoods, Douglas fir, Sitka spruce, and Port Orford cedars stood. (These, it should be noted, still exist in forests protected by private owners and states as well as by federal policies.) But it was also true in the piney wood belts of Georgia, Alabama, Mississippi, and Louisiana. This habitat of soft-fiber trees provided pulpwood for paper products. In addition, the hardwood stands in the middle and upper Midwest were treated with trivial carelessness by today's standards, as great forests were harvested to construct office buildings, bridges, highways, and homes, or burned to clear fields for agriculture.

Yet it is unfair to judge these actions by modern criteria. Cutting forests was not a wanton, foolish action in the last century.

The nation was expanding, a vigorous population was moving westward under the publicly held doctrine of Manifest Destiny to populate the entire continent from the Atlantic to the Pacific Ocean. Was it shortsighted to cut, clear, and burn forests to make room for an energetic population? If salmon choked your streams, would it be unreasonable or wrong to catch more than you could consume and use the excess to fertilize fruit trees or fields of grain?

Today, of course, the answer would be an unequivocal yes. But today salmon are in short supply, while we have an abundance of other fertilizers. In the nineteenth century, the answer would have been an equally unequivocal no for the reverse reasons.

You cannot in fairness judge today's environmental needs by yesterday's standards. Yesterday's liberal who cut down trees to build a log cabin is not the same as today's liberal who would never fell a tree in order to conserve a forest, even when it is no longer necessary to national survival. This is not to say forests should be razed; on the contrary, they should be preserved—but within limits that recognize the needs of a modern population. We cannot go back to the nineteenth century. Not unless we wish to live with no automotive power, no electricity, no microwaves or home garbage disposals, no refrigerators or thermostatically controlled home heating. If we wish to live in the twentieth century, we must pay a price. And part of that price is burning hydrocarbon fuels.

In the westward expansion of the American continent, it was necessary to tame the wilderness so human beings living at the marginal edge of existence could ranch, mine, hunt, build cities, and create a better life for themselves. What happened in the nineteenth century was not so much an indifference to the environment as an effort to provide for a growing population. When survival was the issue, as it was then, anyone attempting to put up barriers against natural resources needed to live, or to improve the national standard of living, would have been resoundingly rejected by the body politic.

In the nineteenth century, where some modern environmentalists tend to stay locked, an apparent disregard for the environment was exhibited by the coal-mining industry when it sought to produce fuel as cheaply and profitably as possible to drive the new industrial economy. As mining technology advanced in the coal-rich regions of Appalachian

Pennsylvania, West Virginia, and Kentucky, strip miners sliced away billions of tons of soil to get at the coal, leaving millions of acres of once-lush mountainside looking like the pitted surface of a lifeless moonscape.[1] As the strip miners' steam-powered shovels retreated, low-lying areas collected water that rippled in cobalt blue beauty, a chimeric illusion only. The same things are occurring today in developing countries; a clean environment is a luxury that only thriving nations can afford.

By today's standards those acts were unconscionable. Yet without that coal, steelmakers in Pennsylvania and auto manufacturers in Detroit would have been unable to flourish. And hundreds of thousands of immigrant families would not have been able to find work. If today's rules had been in effect, the increased cost of coal would have slowed America's economic growth and condemned millions of people to lives of poverty.

The petroleum industry was no different from logging or coal mining in its infancy. As rich oilfields were discovered and drilled in the first years of the twentieth century, wildcatters permitted wells to gush for weeks before being capped, because well-control technology hadn't caught up with drilling. Whatever the reason, the oil seeped through the ground and poisoned subsurface water supplies. This was especially true in East Texas, where the 75,000-barrel per day Spindletop field, discovered in 1901, gushed for days before being capped. Some of this oil was recovered and sold, but it was not a high priority. At 3 cents a barrel—the selling price at the time—it was more economical to let the crude petroleum that shot into the air collect in pools than to pump it into containers for refining. Simple economics dictated many of the practices we would not condone today.

As the huge fields of West Texas were found and developed, moreover, the natural gas was sometimes permitted to escape and burn off at a rate of millions of cubic feet per day for months, sometimes years, on end. Natural gas is a "clean" fuel, but early drillers regarded it as a pesky nuisance that had no real commercial value, an unwelcome byproduct of black gold. No one worried about environmental damage. At that time, most U.S. communities pumped raw sewage into nearby lakes or streams for many of the same reasons energy and mineral development was handled as it was: economics, primarily, and lack of environmental awareness. All attention was focused upon new ways of utilizing the energy for the public good—which did not include environmental purity.

In a way, this seemingly thoughtless damage to the environment in the early years reflected the energetic people building a robust industrial civilization. But it also revealed something important about extractive industries. Taking natural resources from the earth is a tough business. Cutting timber, digging for coal, or drilling for oil are jobs that do not attract poets or artists. These hardy people do not tend to place a priority on the beauty of a bird's flight or a golden wildflower's struggle to plant roots in rocky soil. In a broad sense, this may explain why as recently as World War II, much of the nation's bitter and bloody labor unrest revolved around the nation's extractive industries.

But the last half of the twentieth century has been different. A number of factors combined to awaken among oil and gas producers an awareness of the importance of the environment. Granted, this didn't come easily for some. But, however reluctantly, they too finally accepted environmental responsibility. They too understood that our postindustrial society objects—and with good reason—to the noise, smoke, and pollutants that accompany industrialization.

The 1960s marked the emergence of the environmental movement as a political force. While much of its political expertise came through effective marketing of the political rhetoric of savvy strategists such as Ralph Nader, who polished his skills in the consumer movement, environmentalists' early victories rested on two developments.

The first was the growing awareness of the hazards of air pollution in such large metropolitan areas as New York City and Los Angeles. This led to the Clean Air Act of 1967, which passed the U.S. Senate overwhelmingly (88–3). In one important consequence, the tougher air-quality standards made it more economical for some public utilities to switch from coal-fired to the less polluting oil-generated electricity.

In retrospect, this backfired—it increased the demand for crude oil. Evidence of the contradiction—and more ammunition for environmentalists to use against the U.S. oil and gas industry—came only two years later. In early 1969, a well in the Santa Barbara channel off

Southern California's scenic shoreline accidentally began discharging huge quantities of oil. It was a curiosity of geology. Oil had been seeping slowly from the site, known as an "anticline," for centuries. But when a drill bit bored into the geological formation, the seepage became a flood. Based on geological knowledge at the time, the accident couldn't have been anticipated with any degree of accuracy. No matter. Before it was halted, about 69,000 barrels of crude oil had sputtered to the surface.[2] Soon, a gummy slick of viscous petroleum began washing ashore to blacken thirty miles of beach front. Newspapers and magazines published grisly pictures of dead waterfowl lying in puddles of oil on the beach. Television news broadcasts broke away from the war in Vietnam to show film clips of volunteers working feverishly to clean up the mess.

All of this was a true picture, however unavoidable the geological accident might have been. (Environmental purists, of course, would say that it could have been avoided by not drilling for oil in the first place. True. But in that event the energy would have been unavailable for national use. What's the balance here? Is the other side of the equation—the cost of *not* drilling for oil and gas—reported accurately?)

The nation was shocked by these graphic pictures of environmental damage, and the Nixon administration declared a moratorium on drilling California's offshore waters. But ironically, as mentioned, this environmentally prompted restriction on drilling came at a time when other environmental pressures were increasing the demand for oil. It is a good example of the schizophrenic attitude of society today—wanting it both ways, environmental purity and sufficient cheap energy.

Contradictions aside, the 1969 drilling ban was a watershed in the struggle between environmentalism and oil production for several reasons. It revealed the discordant environmental goals—producing oil and meeting consumers' demands for more cheap petroleum products. This meant oil and gas companies had to spend huge sums of money to protect fragile environments. Most of these costs were ultimately, of course, passed along to consumers. In 1990, the U.S. petroleum industry spent a total of $7.8 billion on direct environmental expenditures, up from approximately $5.8 billion (adjusted for inflation) six years earlier. Of the 1990 total, $2.7 billion went for prevention of water pollution, $2.2 billion to cut down on air pollution, and the remainder for removing nonproducing facilities, managing solid wastes, and handling other collateral activities.

Another result was the dissipation of cash that otherwise could have been used to increase domestic oil and gas production.

And this leads to another contradiction born of the 1969 offshore California drilling moratorium: reducing U.S. supplies to protect the environment has meant rising imports. And almost all of these imports are by water-borne tankers. Which means ever-increasing risks of major spills from foreign tankers that do not subscribe to the same standards of safety followed by U.S. flag vessels. This helps explain why the oil-spill rate in U.S. waters rose in 1990 to 1.8 spills per billion ton miles from an average of 1.6 spills per billion ton miles in the 1980s. (A "ton mile" is the equivalent of transporting one ton of crude oil one mile.)

The Coast Guard estimates that 20 gallons of oil are spilled for each million gallons of oil imported. In 1990, the United States imported approximately 2.15 billion barrels of oil. Thus, almost 50,000 barrels of coastal petroleum spillage occurred in 1990 as a direct result of imports. This is a 25 percent increase over import spillage in 1980.

The 1969 drilling prohibition presented the nation with this knotty little equation: *Reducing domestic drilling to protect the environment leads to greater imports and a higher risk of domestic spills, which brings even greater environmental damage from foreign suppliers.*

A few other points should be made about the environmental risk of oil spills and the petroleum industry's role therein:

1. Only about 60 percent of the approximately 2.1 million barrels of crude oil and petroleum products spilled into U.S. waters between 1980 and 1990 were directly related to the industry's activities. The remaining 40 percent—or more than 800,000 barrels—was spilled by the U.S. government and its armed forces, other industries, and private citizens.

2. Most of the spills recorded in the decade of the 1980s were so minor as to pose absolutely no immediate or permanent threat to

human, animal, or plant life—80 percent of the spills totaled 50 gallons or less.

3. A few exceptionally large, well-publicized spills distorted the overall performance record and the public's perception—in 1989, for example, the *Exxon Valdez* discharge represented more than 75 percent of all oil spilled by U.S. energy companies that year, and in 1990, the *Mega Borg*'s 93,000-barrel spill off the Texas Gulf coast accounted for more than half of all that year's pollution by oil spillage worldwide.

A second reason the 1969 drilling ban was a watershed was that it was the first in a long series of drilling prohibitions. As their movement acquired more political clout, radical leaders of the environmental movement did not stand idly by.

They rushed to obtain court injunctions, not just to prohibit pumping oil and gas from areas supposedly damaging to the environment, but to stop exploratory drilling which would determine whether oil and gas even existed. Indeed, the emphasis subtly shifted from the danger of spills to human beings, to this or that danger to nonhuman life forms. Today, the emphasis is on barring exploration efforts, not production.

If the environmental leaders cannot convince through arguing about the hazards to humans from exploration and development, they switch ground and speak of seals, aquatic fowl, and other wildlife. These relentless attacks are making the U.S. oil and gas industry—especially the independents, which have found most of the energy deposits—more of an endangered specie than any on the environmentalists' list.

One of Abe Phillips' first land acquisitions after becoming president of Coors Energy Co. in 1979 was a lease to drill on four thousand acres of rocky, mountainous soil in Southeastern Utah.

Phillips, born in Oklahoma in 1924, has spent virtually his entire life in the oil and gas industry. He worked in the oilfields to finance his education in petroleum geology at the University of Oklahoma and, upon graduating in 1949, joined Exxon Corp. as a geologist. He spent seven of his thirty years with them overseas and became manager of Exxon's Western Division before joining the energy company owned by the Coors beer family in Colorado.

Based on Phillips' experience, the federally owned Lost Canyon tract near Moab, Utah, looked like an ideal spot for oil exploration. The land was rugged and unpopulated, a starkly beautiful blend of mountains and desert, canyons and mesas, with a railroad line running within a half mile of the tract. Phillips found evidence of oil in rocky outcroppings, and suggestions in the visible geological formations that pools of oil and gas lay below. Phillips committed Coors to paying $400,000 to the federal government for a lease to drill the property at some point in the future, with the lease renewable yearly for $1 an acre. Over a ten-year period, Coors paid the federal treasury an additional $40,000, or a total of $440,000, for rights to drill on the property.

In 1990, Phillips directed a seismic crew to begin sounding the depths for oil and gas. The crew estimated that the Lost Canyon tract contained 25 million barrels of recoverable oil, and Coors applied to the Bureau of Land Management for a permit to drill. But the Southern Utah Wilderness Alliance, a coalition of environmental groups, went to federal court in Salt Lake City and got a temporary injunction prohibiting drilling on the site. The environmentalists argued that such drilling would endanger a herd of big-horn sheep that inhabited the area.

But Phillips, who thought the number of sheep had been exaggerated, persuaded Coors to hire its own biologist to study the area and make a physical head count of the big-horn population. The biologist discovered that no more than ten big-horn sheep roamed the mountains, and not all of these were on the Lost Canyon tract.

Meanwhile, the federal Bureau of Land Management, which was responsible for the tract, hired a second biologist to study the big-horn sheep controversy. As Gene Nodine, former executive director of the Bureau of Land Management in Utah, explained, the BLM's philosophy was to issue oil and gas leases to allow people to drill, not to stop them because of phony claims. "The environmentalists," Nodine told us, "were obstructionists" in the Lost Canyon dispute.

But the potential harm arising from the controversy was too much for Coors. The family made its money brewing beer, not drilling for oil. And they lived in Colorado, where environmental consciousness is acute. No purpose would be served if the beer company got tangled up in a street fight with environmentalists over ten big-horn sheep. The company sold its leases and walked away.

The results?

According to Phillips, the company planned to drill up to eight production wells if its first wildcat struck oil. With crews of twenty workers per rig, this added up to some 160 unrealized jobs.

At $20 a barrel, the Lost Canyon tract could have produced $500 million worth of oil. This would have benefitted not only the Coors Energy Co., but its investors. Over the producing life of the tract, some $500 million would have been added to our Gross National Product and reduced our dependence on foreign oil producers by 25 million barrels.

Moreover, the area was denied several million dollars in unrealized property and other local taxes. "The schools need money," says Moab Mayor Tom Stocks. "It [drilling the Lost Canyon tract] would have helped." Some who live in Moab do not want the Lost Canyon tract developed because they prefer isolation. That's understandable. Even so, it would have been an economic boon for the community.

Finally, although the big-horn sheep were saved from the inconvenience of sharing their habitat with eight drilling rigs—about one for every five hundred acres, on average—they were not saved from the rifles of hunters. According to the Utah Department of Wildlife Resources, the Lost Canyon sheep were included as game when hunting licenses were sold in 1991 ($200 for Utah residents, $1,000 for nonresidents). Why? Because they were not endangered; on the contrary, they were plentiful.

So, in the final analysis, we traded $500 million worth of oil for a maximum of $10,000 in fees from hunting licenses (assuming there were ten sheep in the Los Canyon vicinity, and assuming all were shot by nonresident hunters). Hunting trophies don't get much more expensive than that.

It would be far less troubling if the Lost Canyon episode were an aberration. Unfortunately, the incident typifies the irresponsible harm being done to millions of Americans today—as well as the generations of tomorrow—by contemporary environmental policies that have less to do with economic reality than with promoting irrational causes.

Look, for example, at federal policies governing plugging and abandoning nonproducing wells. Until recently, federal regulations required that all exhausted wells—whether onshore or offshore—be plugged and abandoned within a year after production ceased. This was to prevent possible seepage and pollution from an inactive well. So far, so good.

But, according to the environmentalists, the rule would not do as applied to offshore drilling and production platforms. It appears that a drilling or production platform creates an artificial underwater barrier, a reef, that encourages development of marine life. The steel pilings and other underwater structures attract plankton, which attract shellfish, which attract larger fish, which attract sport fishing and fishing fleets, which employ people and generate economic wealth.

Offshore drilling platforms thus actually enhance the marine environment. And this has frustrated radical environmentalists who believe that *all* exploration and production of oil and gas is environmentally harmful. It is a knotty dilemma: the federal laws that require drillers to remove offshore drilling and production structures once the energy beneath is exhausted also require them to destroy a delicate marine ecosystem.

And so the environmentalists did their thing, and today the government allows oil and gas producers to tow an unusable drilling platform and sink it in approved areas to create artificial "rig reefs" in order to improve the quality of the marine environment.

Another interesting contradiction: The state of Florida encourages drillers to abandon marine drilling equipment off the state's beaches to enhance and multiply marine life along the coast. Yet the state militates against drilling for energy in the potentially rich fields that lie offshore from Pensacola in the Panhandle along the Gulf and Atlantic coastlines to St. Augustine in North Florida.

All of which goes to prove once again that, as Abraham Lincoln observed, when people say it's the principle and not personal gain that motivates them, it's usually not the principle.

Another example of how unrealistic environmental considerations impede the domestic industry revolve around what environmentalists call "hazardous wastes."

To begin with, "hazardous waste" is an emotional phrase that triggers certain images. It conjures mental pictures of gooey green slime, lead contamination, and toxic substances that turn children into freakish creatures with twisted bodies and burned-out minds.

Today, despite the billions of dollars the oil and gas industry has spent and is spending each year on environmental protection, drilling mud and other exploration fluids are being characterized as "hazardous wastes." Drilling mud isn't gooey green slime or "hazardous waste" by anybody's definition. To understand the absurdity of this argument, it is necessary to go back in time for a moment.

In 1980, Congress specifically exempted drilling muds and certain other exploration and production sweepings from hazardous-waste provisions of the Resource Conservation and Recovery Act. This exemption was made for several reasons: (1) most of these wastes were not "hazardous" by any leap of the imagination; and (2) most of the wastes were already managed in a manner that complied with all existing state and federal regulations—tough regulations that, in the past decade, have been strengthened even further. Between 1987 and 1991, Oklahoma added more than thirty new rules governing oil and gas waste management; Louisiana has required more cementing of wellsite holes to protect water tables; and West Virginia, Montana, Alabama, and New Mexico have adopted more stringent guidelines for exploration production waste management.

Oil and gas companies have worked hard to comply with the regulations. In Alaska—one of the environmentalists' target areas for study and criticism—drilling wastes are injected into wells as deep as two thousand feet. This is far below the environmentally fragile frozen tundra, which extends only about three to six inches beneath the surface of Arctic soil.

But such efforts are of little consequence to environmental extremists. Today, a campaign is underway to have drilling muds and other exploration by-products classified as "hazardous" because they contain almost untraceable radioactive materials.

"Radioactive" is yet another buzzword designed to raise people's hair. No one denies that drilling muds and other fluids that are pumped into the earth acquire tiny amounts of radioactive contamination from contact with deep-earth soil. This phenomenon was first noticed in the former Soviet Union in the 1930s. But there is nothing sinister or strange about it. Radium and other radioactive materials exist in virtually all subsurface geological structures, such as backyards where shovels are likely to pick up minute traces of radioactive contamination. The question is not whether subsurface radioactivity exists; it is rather whether radioactive contamination of drilling muds and other exploration fluids poses a danger to surface soil and water, and hence to humans and wildlife.

The answer is an unequivocal no.

Surveys have demonstrated that more than 99 percent of the radioactive materials drawn to the surface by oil and gas production facilities are less than one-third the allowable limits set by the U.S. Occupational Health and Safety Administration. And this low level of risk is reduced even further by industry standards that require systematic flushing of extraction and production equipment and other safety rules.

Yet environmental extremists are seeking to have such oil and gas wastes subjected to the same regulations as other industrial byproducts, a clear case of comparing apples and oranges. If this should occur, the results would be disastrous. According to a study made by Gruy Engineering Corp. for the American Petroleum Institute:

- More than 500,000 oil wells in the United States would have to be shut down;
- Another 200,000 domestic natural gas wells would be plugged and production halted;
- U.S. oil production would decline by about 440 million barrels a year, or almost 20 percent of total current domestic production, thus further increasing our dependence on foreign suppliers;
- Some 40,000 more American oil and gas workers would lose their jobs, as would at least another 100,000 workers in industries that supply the business;

- State and local property and severance tax revenues would decline by almost $1 billion *in the first year alone.*

The radical leadership in the environmental movement is killing the golden goose in two ways: First, by imposing unnecessary and unrealistic health and safety standards that have little to do with health and safety but much to do with emotional hand-wringing, and second, by limiting areas where U.S. independent oil and gas companies, such as Coors Energy, can look for new pools of energy.

As previously mentioned, almost a third of the United States is owned by the federal government, most of it in the West in Alaska, Oregon, California, Nevada, and Arizona. Huge supplies of gas and oil lie beneath these federal lands. They lie dormant because the opponents of drilling seem to prefer increasing our dependence on foreign oil to allowing us to dig for the riches beneath our own soil. It is difficult to avoid concluding that their agenda is ultimately to stop all oil consumption.

As proof, look at how they have blocked drilling in the Arctic National Wildlife Refuge. And this has happened at a time when the nation is becoming dangerously dependent on foreign energy. We have even gone to war (Desert Shield and Desert Storm), at least in part, to protect oilfields in the Middle East.

A bitter irony is evident here: We're willing to endanger the lives of young Americans to protect foreign oil supplies. At the same time, we do not develop our own energy reserves in order to protect an already adequately protected caribou population. We want cheap energy. But how many Porcupine River Arctic caribou—which are not at risk anyway—are worth the life of a single U.S. soldier, sailor, airplane pilot, or Marine? Wild animals and fragile plants are creations of God. But so too are men and women.

Alaska's overall environment has not been permanently damaged by oil exploration and development of the North Slope fields. Nor is it likely that any irreparable harm would be done to the equally rich deposits that almost certainly lie beneath a small portion of the Arctic National Wildlife Refuge territory. The question then becomes this:

Are we willing as a nation to take a calculated risk to explore these fields, knowing that the potential danger to the environment is small; or do we not do so, knowing that this puts the nation in perilous dependence on foreign oil. The answer to this is the record on drilling for oil and gas in Alaska, and the potential represented by energy deposits that lie beneath Alaska's frozen tundra.

CHAPTER FIVE

NORTH TO ALASKA

PRUDHOE BAY AND THE ARCTIC
NATIONAL WILDLIFE REFUGE

As Under Secretary and Secretary of the Department of the Interior and Secretary of the Department of Energy between 1981 to 1989, one of my major responsibilities was to encourage the exploration and development of the potentially oil-rich Arctic National Wildlife Refuge.

By 1985, I had become alarmed at the fall in oil prices that was devastating our ability to produce our own basic energy resources profitably and increasing our reliance on foreign sources. I had seen employment in the industry drop precipitously, and scores of independent oil and gas producers, as well as their suppliers, march into bankruptcy court. At about this time, the immense oil resources of the Arctic National Wildlife Refuge became a cause of controversy.

On a couple of occasions, I went to the North Slope of Alaska to give U.S. representatives and senators first-hand views of the area. We visited Kaktovik, a village set squarely in the middle of the coastline of a small area that could produce billions of barrels of oil, if geological estimates are accurate. The drilling platform where the first test well was bored was intact, made of wood decking on about two feet of styrofoam insulation. The insulation prevented thawing of the permafrost beneath the rig so the delicate soil would not be scarred when the platform was removed.

The area I saw was impressive, but not in a way you might imagine. It was bleak, flat, and frigid beyond belief. I wondered how people could work there in the winter, when temperatures combined with the wind to produce chill factors of 100 degrees below zero or worse. And I wondered how workers could drill a seismic hole without leaving marks such as those found years after oil exploration crews left the sage brush or other desert areas where energy was often discovered. (In Alaska, the only signs of man came from the Defense Early Warning, or DEW, System constructed by the U.S. and Canada decades earlier.)

When I next visited the Kaktovik well site about two years later, we hoped to show congressional visitors the "impact" of drilling after the initial platform had been removed. Several of our visitors had trouble even recognizing the site only a few hundred feet below our helicopter. After alighting, we stood at the edge of what less than twenty-four months earlier had been a full-blown drilling site. If no one had told us, we would never have known. The only proof that we were at the right spot was a section of drill pipe that had been left, thrusting a few feet out of the ground, to mark the location of the well.

One of the senators, known as "an environmentalist," finally asked, "What's all the fuss about?" But that moment of rational insight didn't last. When it came time to vote on opening the Arctic National Wildlife Refuge to oil exploration and development, the political realities of an environmental movement that is more evangelical than rational overcame that honest reaction.

—Donald Paul Hodel

Most students of U.S. history regard President Thomas Jefferson's 1803 acquisition of 827,192 square miles of mostly unexplored territory as the nation's premier real estate deal. There is no question in modern eyes that the Louisiana Purchase was a bargain-basement transaction. For a total of $18 million—a little more than $18 per square mile—the United States acquired title to an enormous tract of land stretching from the Gulf of Mexico to the Canadian border. It included the future states of Louisiana, Oklahoma, Missouri, Iowa, Minnesota, Wisconsin, Kansas, Nebraska, Colorado, Wyoming, and both Dakotas. For less than 30 cents per acre, the United States acquired the expansive granaries of the Middle West, much of the stately Rocky Mountains region, and the enormous pools of oil and gas created millions of years ago when oceans covered much of today's Oklahoma, Kansas, Nebraska, and Colorado.

Jefferson got a bargain. He set the stage for Secretary of State William Seward's acquisition of Alaska in 1868 from the Imperial Russian government. Reduced to its essentials, Seward, like Jefferson, cut a deal of jumbo proportions for the United States. And like the Louisiana Purchase in earlier days, much of Alaska remains raw unpopulated land. Again like the Louisiana Purchase, Alaska's energy reserves are immense. For a mere $7.2 million, Seward quietly purchased almost 600,000 square miles of raw territory—384 million acres of forest, fishing and hunting territory, and frozen tundra teeming with wildlife, gold deposits, and incredibly abundant oil and gas stockpiles. Although contemporary critics called the transaction "Seward's Folly," the potential riches are mind-boggling.

The wisdom of Seward's purchase was made evident only a year after Alaska became U.S. territory, when veins of gold were discovered near Nome in 1869. But those deposits, along with the plentiful Klondike gold lode found thirty years later, were nothing compared with the oil and gas wealth that was discovered in the 1960s.

Wildcatters sensed the presence of oil and gas in Alaska as early as the 1920s. In fact, President Warren Harding established a naval petroleum reserve on the western Arctic coast in 1923.[1]

But not until the 1960s did the extent of Alaska's oil and gas wealth on the North Slope near Prudhoe Bay become evident to geophysicists and geologists exploring the area. After numerous wildcatting expeditions, a joint venture of ARCO and Humble Oil finally hit pay dirt the day after Christmas 1967. The dramatic moment was described by Pulitzer Prize-winning author and oil analyst Daniel Yergin in *THE PRIZE*. He wrote:

"On December 26, 1967, a loud, vibrating sound drew a crowd of about 40 men to the [Prudhoe Bay exploration] well. They were wrapped in heavy clothes—it was thirty degrees below zero—and they had to struggle to hold their places in the thirty-knot wind. The noise grew louder and louder—the roar of natural gas. To one geologist it sounded like four jumbo jets flying directly overhead. A natural gas flare from a pipe shot defiantly thirty feet straight up in the strong wind. They had struck oil. . . ."[2] This well had been preceded by more than six dry holes, but it was followed by other discoveries that paid rich dividends. And, by 1968, it was clear that the Prudhoe Bay field was the largest ever discovered on the North American continent. Indeed, it even surpassed the legendary East Texas fields found in the early 1900s when the Spindletop well forever changed the nature of the U.S. oil industry. With recoverable reserves of more than an estimated 9 billion barrels of oil, the North Shore deposits at Prudhoe Bay were one of the largest fields ever found, surpassed in size only by single-field reservoirs in oil-rich Saudi Arabia and Kuwait.

But the timing for development of the North Shore field was unfortunate. The discovery roughly coincided with the smog alerts that had led to the 1967 Clean Air Act, and the 1969 Santa Barbara oil blowout that energized the young environmental movement. As a result, the Cassandras of environmental gloom and doom mustered their forces and fought the development of the North Slope's oil and gas.

The environmental movement focused its efforts on preventing construction of the Trans-Alaska pipeline, an eight hundred-mile conduit of forty-eight-inch tubing projected to run from Prudhoe Bay on the North Slope to Valdez abutting Prince William Sound on Alaska's Pacific coastline. With Prudhoe Bay locked in ice most of the year, and no roadways running from the newly discovered oilfield south, it was necessary to find a way of transporting the crude oil other than by tanker.

Numerous alternatives were explored. According to Yergin in THE PRIZE, the options considered ran from the unlikely (construction of an eight-lane highway) to the patently absurd (nuclear-powered submarine tankers that would be filled at a new deep-water port created by a nuclear explosion). They dreaded the only realistic alternative: a pipeline. The environmentalists knew that preventing construction of a pipeline would effectively shut down development of the Prudhoe Bay Field. The strategy was effective and later adopted by other environmental leaders.

In any event, by 1968, the consortium of oil companies that had explored the North Slope field was ready to begin constructing a pipeline to transport the huge quantities of oil. Then, in January 1969, the Santa Barbara blowout occurred. It was just the ammunition environmentalist opponents needed to halt work on the pipeline. They went to court to seek an injunction, and successfully argued that the pipeline would irreparably damage the delicate permafrost subsurface of the Arctic soil. As originally planned, putting the entire pipeline underground would have created a melt-freeze cycle that would have damaged the permafrost layer. But this problem was solved by placing pads of gravel beneath the subsurface pipeline structure.

New objections were raised. The pipeline would interrupt the migratory patterns of the caribou herd. Lawyers for the environmentalists painted false pictures of how herds of caribou would be dislocated, their grazing treks across the tundra interrupted leaving most either to die of starvation or be so weakened as to fall prey to ravenous wolves. Nor was this all. Once the caribou were gone, the wolves and other predators that feed on them would die. The Arctic food chain would have irreparably broken links, the argument continued, and Alaskan life, perhaps life on the entire globe, would be permanently, catastrophically altered. And all because of a pipeline the big oil companies wanted to reap their immense profits!

The court was moved. An injunction against building the pipeline was issued in the late 1960s, and there it remained until 1973, when the OPEC oil embargo changed people's minds. In 1973 legislation was passed under the leadership of Senator Henry M. (Scoop) Jackson of Washington, which lifted the ban, and construction of the Trans-Alaska pipeline began. It would take four years to complete. To comply with environmental concerns, the pipeline was raised above the tundra in some places to protect the delicate permafrost and, in others, it was elevated to permit the free passage of caribou. Oil did not start flowing until 1977. Within a year, 1 million barrels of oil were pulsing through the pipeline each day. By the early 1980s volume had increased to 2 million barrels a day—fully 25 percent of the nation's daily production.[3]

The environmental impact of oil and gas development in Alaska can today be judged from the vantage point of more than a decade. In brief, the impact has been, by several significant measurements, favorable.

Granted, this will be disputed by environmentalists. But they point largely to the *Exxon Valdez* disaster while often ignoring the other part of the record. The fact remains—the damage that environmentalists warned would occur if Prudhoe Bay oil were transported south via pipeline has simply not come about.

Take the wildlife issue. The environmentalists contended that the pipeline would severely damage, if not wholly destroy, the Central Arctic caribou herd. This emotional argument has great appeal for all of us. Arctic caribou are equated with reindeer, Santa's animal helpers. The caribou, though antlered, are a nonthreatening quadruped that migrate into and beyond the Brooks Mountain range in winter, and graze the tundra of the North Slope in summer. The environmentalists claimed that the caribou would become mired hock-deep in the melting permafrost when they traversed soil warmed to the gluey paste that the underground pipeline, carrying hot crude oil, would create. So immobilized, the caribou would either starve to death or be easy prey for the wolves and bear that scavange the tundra.

The pleadings were groundless, a fact demonstrated by scientific evidence. In 1990, a biological census of the Central Arctic herd revealed that the caribou population near and around Prudhoe Bay totaled about eighteen thousand animals—a *sixfold* increase from the three thousand caribou counted in 1970. In fact, the herd has so increased that, like Utah's big-horn sheep, they can now be safely harvested. The facts contradict assertions that oil and gas companies have no regard for the natural state of the places where they drill and pump energy. Several other environmental claims have been proved equally erroneous.

Nor is the protection of the caribou population the only environmental benefit that has resulted from oil and gas production in Alaska. We were told, for example, that the *Exxon Valdez* oil spill was a "100-year disaster." Wrong again. Granted the oil spill was harmful to the environment—but only temporarily. Granted, too, that there was more serious temporary damage done to the local fishing industry. But within a few short years, certainly an insignificant moment in geological time, Prince William Sound will be as pristine as ever, according to some environmental study groups.

Exxon Corporation paid about $1.1 billion in fines for the *Valdez* spill, and committed another $25 million to clean up the mess. In contrast, the value of the oil spilled was only about $14 million. The impact of Exxon's efforts is already evident. Independent studies indicate that the last traces of the oil spill will be gone before the end of this decade. Moreover, the clean-up efforts have expanded environmental knowledge and technology and produced more efficient safeguards to protect against such accidents in the future.

The *Exxon Valdez* incident has already resulted in federal legislation requiring double-hulled oil tankers by the year 2010. The oil and gas industry has responded positively; in early 1993, a Mobil Oil scientist was given a patent for adapting current fleets to double-hulled configurations for about $35 million less than it would cost to build new ships. This is no small matter when you remember that environmental cleanups and pollution-prevention efforts are ultimately paid by consumers, not oil companies.

Next, we were told by critics of the pipeline that breaks in the pipeline would release tons of oil, hundreds of thousands of barrels, onto the permafrost and devastate the tundra, harming not only grazing caribou but other wildlife as well.

It never happened. According to the state of Alaska, about 700 million barrels of oil and liquid natural gas were pumped through the Trans-Alaska pipeline in 1989. The total accidental spillage that year was about 7,000 barrels. (Most media reports prefer to compute oil spillages in gallons rather than barrels, presumably because oil spillage reported in millions of gallons rather than thousands of barrels is much more dramatic.) That is an insignificant 1/1000th of 1 percent— about the same percentage of oil put into a swimming pool if someone jumped in without first showering off tanning lotion.

Another argument held that the oil and gas furnaces and vehicles at the North Slope production site would spew pollution into the air. Again, this alarm has proved to be illusory, even misleading. In fact, the North Slope air quality is far better than national standards require. The largest volume of air pollutants generated by oil production is nitrogen dioxide, a toxic gas that is created whenever air combines with fuel to burn any type of combustible material. Oxygen molecules combine with the nitrogeneous elements that constitute 78 percent of our atmosphere. Monitoring nitrogen dioxide is a major responsibility assigned to the federal Environmental Protection Agency, and it is done constantly in major oil-producing areas.

The verdict after more than fifteen years is that the monthly average of nitrogen dioxide concentration downwind from Prudhoe Bay is about 15 micrograms per cubic meter of air. This is one-sixth the standard allowed by National Ambient Air Quality standards. You inhale more nitrogen dioxide standing outside the Sierra Club's Washington, D.C., headquarters than on a production pad at Prudhoe Bay. The Sierra Club and its companion organizations would have you believe otherwise. Granted, a number of environmentalists argue with some validity that urban areas should not be compared with virgin wilderness. But it raises the question: what is more important to environmentalists? Human life in urban settings? Or animal life in areas with natural resources capable of making our urban life more comfortable, affordable, and secure? The puzzle is perplexing, and gets to the heart of environmental cost-benefit considerations.

And, finally, there's the matter of disposing of drilling wastes. This is an important topic, because it applies to U.S. oil and gas production areas everywhere. As noted earlier, extremists in the environmental movement are seeking to have drilling mud and other fluids extracted from well sites classified as "hazardous waste" under definitions used to dispose of industrial toxic byproducts and regulations that govern municipal landfills. Even the federal Environmental Protection Agency believes existing regulations governing the disposal of drilling wastes are sufficient to protect air, ground, and water quality. In a 1987 study, the EPA concluded, "When managed in accordance with existing state and federal requirements, exempt oil and gas wastes rarely pose significant threats to human health and the environment."

To regulate drilling waste in this manner would be disastrous to a domestic oil and gas industry already crippled by tax policies and other needless health and safety regulations. Imposing these unnecessary waste-removal regulations would stop almost all new drilling and shut down 80 percent of the nation's producing oil wells and 75 percent of its gas wells, decreasing our already shrinking domestic reserves by another 2.5 billion barrels of oil and 10.3 trillion cubic feet of gas.[4]

Moreover, tough federal requirements have been supplemented by equally and ever more stringent state environmental regulations. And the oil industry has complied—at a price. For example, in Louisiana in March 1991, state regulators approved a rule that required closing all oil industry brine discharges into coastal regions other than open bays and offshore currents. This cost the oil industry almost $1 billion. Similar rules were adopted to control drilling wastes in West Virginia, Texas, Montana, Wyoming, and Colorado. The industry is and for many years has been willing to make financial and operating adjustments in order to comply with public policies that demand a clean environment. But keep in mind that the billions of dollars spent on environmental concerns might otherwise have been employed to find more oil and gas demanded by an energy-dependent society.

This dilemma has special application today in Alaska, which holds an important opportunity for the future of the U.S. oil and gas industry. It might be well to examine how drilling wastes on Alaska's North Slope are handled under state and federal regulations.

Most drilling byproducts consist of water. At Prudhoe Bay, this water is injected in wells that reach as far as two thousand feet beneath the surface of the earth—so deep that no possible damage can be done to the soil-thawing zone (from eighteen inches to three feet below the surface) which undergoes a transition from hard freeze to melt and then back to hard freeze once each year. Moreover, the deep-well water injection level is at the bottom of the permafrost belt—the permanently frozen soil that extends as much as two thousand feet below the surface. Thus the deep-well injections do not endanger the water, which collects on the surface during summer thaws and can be used safely by plants, animals, or humans.

The North Slope of Alaska is a vast expanse of land that slopes gently northward (thus, "North Slope") from the Brooks Mountain range to the Arctic Ocean. It is divided south-to-north from time to time by "ribbon" streams that rush downward from the mountains. The landscape begins with occasional scrub brush at the base of the Brooks Mountain flora line that changes rapidly to tundra. Soon the tundra is marked by peculiar, square-shaped frost cracks on the surface as it nears the ocean. In the summer, you find ponds and shallow lakes. An air traveler has difficulty determining whether the surface below is land with many ponds and lakes, or water with many islands and peninsulas. It is the Arctic Ocean, which even in June is still covered with ice or blocks of ice churned up on the shoreline.

It is a bleak area, and difficult to imagine as the site of potential oil and gas deposits of incredible size. A small portion of this area consists of twenty-three geological formations, each of which could be as large or larger than the multi-billion barrel Prudhoe Bay field. Certainly not all—perhaps none—of these formations contain oil and gas. But they have the potential. Geological studies indicate that the chances of finding a field of truly mammoth proportions are real.

—DONALD PAUL HODEL

The Arctic National Wildlife Refuge is critical to the future of the nation's energy industry. It is therefore important to counteract some of the arguments the environmentalists are using, thus far successfully, to block exploration of the huge energy supplies believed to lie beneath the North Slope area to the east of Prudhoe Bay.

Keep in mind that the Arctic National Wildlife Refuge cannot be considered an isolated portion of Alaska, a serene island. In every way—geologically, geographically, and culturally (wherever humans can be found in the wildlife refuge)—the region being considered for petroleum exploration is linked to the production zone at nearby Prudhoe Bay. As the federal Bureau of Land Management reported in a 1991 study, "It appeared more appropriate to consider the . . . area as part of the North Slope oil province, rather than a rank wildcat frontier. . . ."[5] With this understanding, let us look at the potential for oil and gas in the wildlife refuge.

The Arctic National Wildlife Refuge was created in 1980 by the Alaska National Interest Lands Conservation Act. It is a huge, barren, virtually unpopulated area, about the size of South Carolina, seventy miles east of the Prudhoe Bay production fields. The floral composition is devoid of color or other conventional beauty, consisting almost entirely of drab patches of lichens and mosses that provide food for the caribou. These in turn feed predators such as bears and wolves. Even the Sierra Club concedes that the wildlife refuge is not fit for human habitation. "There is no denying that the coastal plain is an inhuman spot, made for caribou and not for bipeds," wrote Paul Rauber, associate editor of *Sierra*, the Sierra Club's glossy magazine, in its January/February 1992 issue.

But the issue is not whether the ANWR coastal plain is worth saving. As we have pointed out, the area can be drilled without harming the overall environment. Rather, the issue is that the plain is believed to have incredibly rich stores of gas and oil. Studies by the U.S. Department of the Interior indicate a 50–50 chance of finding as much as 9.2 billion barrels of recoverable oil in the area.

Some more optimistic estimates, including one by Robert Gunn, past president of the American Association of Petroleum Geologists, predict that between 15 billion and 30 billion barrels of oil are locked in the coastal plain geological formations. In testimony before a congressional committee in July 1991, Gunn said the Arctic National Wildlife Refuge "is the most promising geological province that I have ever studied. Please be assured that, if opened and if exploration is successful, [the Arctic National Wildlife Refuge] will have a profound effect on our nation's economic and geopolitical structure for many years to come."[6] Gunn says the government's estimate of 9.2 billion barrels of oil is low. And he offered this estimate although private industry geologists must be more cautious than government bureaucrats in making predictions. After all, private industry has to provide the billions of dollars in up-front money required to explore and put a field into production. Therefore Gunn's estimate of 15 billion to 30 billion barrels of oil reserves must be regarded as conservative.

Gunn also told Congress that he believed 14.7 billion barrels of recoverable oil was "unconditional." Moreover, he said, "as additional well control and detailed seismic [studies] become available, the volume of recoverable oil will exceed 15 billion barrels . . . [and] these computations do not include natural [gas] liquids." The "conservative volume" of estimated gas reserves on the Alaska coastal plain, Gunn went on, represents about 18 percent of existing U.S. total natural gas reserves. These are phenomenal numbers. If true, they have enormous political consequences.

Unexplored potential reservoirs of energy of this magnitude almost certainly could be crucial to our national security and the future of our domestic energy supplies. Gunn put the entire problem in a nutshell when he said to Congress: "In my mind, our economy and national security are more fragile than the ecosystems of a minute portion of the Arctic Coastal Plain."

According to the U.S. Department of Energy, 9.2 billion barrels of oil could provide as much as 25 percent of current U.S. production. Each barrel of oil would mean one less barrel purchased abroad, reducing the total trade deficit over a period of time by almost $200 billion (based on an average price of $20 per barrel). The coastal plain field could add to our proven reserves by somewhere between 30 and 40 percent, thus reducing our bondage to the volatile petropolitics of the Middle East.[7]

The economic impact of developing the Arctic National Wildlife Refuge would have a ripple effect that would benefit every state in the union. In Alaska, developing the field would spark billions of dollars in new investment. In developing the Prudhoe Bay field, oil companies spent more than $47 billion putting the oilfield into production. This money went to every state in the Union, for drilling equipment, services, consultants, and so on.

Wharton Econometrics Forecasting Associates constructed a computer model of the job growth potential of the Coastal Plain oilfield and determined that more than 732,000 *new* jobs would be created nationwide by the year 2005 by opening up the new find. Virtually every sector of the economy would benefit, Wharton concluded, with most of the new jobs generated in such industries as food, textiles, apparel, paper, refining, rubber and plastics, wood and lumber, stone, clay and glass, primary and fabricated metals, machinery, transportation, construction, and financial services. According to the Wharton computer model, the number of jobs that would be created in each state by the year 2005 would be:

STATE	ESTIMATED NEW JOBS, 2005
Alaska	12,795
Alabama	10,392
Arkansas	5,464
Arizona	10,447
California	79,793
Colorado	10,577
Connecticut	10,989
Delaware	2,032
District of Columbia	2,516
Florida	33,878
Georgia	18,374
Hawaii	2,702
Idaho	2,369
Iowa	6,662
Illinois	33,375
Indiana	15,622
Kansas	7,183
Kentucky	12,247
Louisiana	14,846
Massachusetts	20,260
Maryland	13,192
Maine	3,450
Michigan	25,014
Minnesota	13,489
Missouri	14,138
Mississippi	5,918
Montana	2,126
North Carolina	19,389
Nebraska	4,006
New Hampshire	3,898
New Jersey	22,046
New Mexico	4,669
Nevada	4,725
New York	47,624
Ohio	31,842

STATE	ESTIMATED NEW JOBS, 2005
Oklahoma	11,268
Oregon	6,885
Pennsylvania	34,279
Rhode Island	2,919
South Carolina	9,421
South Dakota	1,771
Tennessee	13,394
Texas	60,168
Utah	4,580
Virginia	19,269
Vermont	1,740
Washington	12,157
Wisconsin	13,814
West Virginia	7,043
Wyoming	2,958
Total	**732,223**

Look for a moment at what opening the coastal plain field could mean for employment in just three states, according to the Wharton model. And keep in mind that almost all of these are well-paid, productive, and professional jobs, not entry level minimum-wage positions tossing hamburgers at a fast-food restaurant.

- **California**: a total of about 80,000 jobs would be created. The state's construction industry would add 16,000 jobs, the services industry 17,000 jobs, and the trade industry (or sales of products) 25,000 jobs. And none of this includes jobs that would not be *lost* in California's extensive shipbuilding and refining industries if the domestic oil and gas industry continues to deteriorate.
- **New Mexico**: about 5,000 jobs would be added to this state, whose population ranks thirty-seventh in the fifty states. These would include 1,700 in the mining (oil and gas extraction) industry, 1,200 in the trading sector, and 1,000 in the construction industry. Moreover, opening the Arctic National Wildlife Refuge would add almost 1 percent to New Mexico's employment base.

- **Oregon**: The environmental movement is strong in Oregon, and understandably so, given the state's natural beauty. No oil is produced in Oregon, although the state consumes about 70 million barrels of petroleum products each year. Yet Oregon would also benefit by development of the Arctic National Wildlife Refuge. The trade sector in Oregon would realize 2,500 new jobs; the construction industry 1,000 jobs; the service industry 1,400 jobs; and the hard-pressed timber industry 780 new jobs.

All of these estimates of new job growth are predicated, of course, on finding 9.2 billion barrels of recoverable oil. The environmentalists try to play this down. But their reasoning is seriously flawed; it is based on assumptions that are ignorant or false.

The Sierra Club, for example, implies that an Interior Department study indicates "that there is a 95 percent chance that the Arctic Refuge contains more than 600 million barrels of oil, and a 5 percent chance that it contains a supergiant 9.2 billion barrel field."[8] In fact, the prospects of finding a giant field are not a mere "5 percent" as the environmentalists would have you believe. The Department of the Interior has reported that professional geologists rate the Arctic National Wildlife Refuge "as the most outstanding petroleum exploration target in the onshore United States," potentially the largest field ever found in the continental United States.[9]

The facts speak for themselves. The Interior Department rates the chances of finding a major discovery on the coastal plain at a remarkably high 46 percent, or about one chance in two. This compares with a hit rate of about 14 percent for most wildcat wells, and only one in seven will reveal a major discovery—more than 1 million barrels of recoverable oil. The Sierra Club and other environmental wardens, moreover, would have you believe the potential of the wildlife refuge field is only about 600 million barrels, despite expert geological estimates. Even if true, 600 million barrels would be a major discovery and worth the almost negligible environmental impact that would ensue.

If the environmental opponents were correct, why would the oil and gas companies spend billions of dollars to develop an uneconomical field? Why spend $22 or $23 a barrel to find oil that sells for only $20?

Any corporate manager who made that kind of decision would get the summary dismissal he or she would have richly earned.

In any case, the only way to find out is through exploration. If huge quantities of recoverable oil lie beneath a minute portion of the Arctic National Wildlife Refuge, surely it is worth searching for. And, in any case, where is the danger in exploratory drilling of one or two, or even six or eight wildcat holes? The amount of land that would be disturbed is minimal. With past performance as a guide, wildlife would suffer no harmful effects. In short, the environmental risks are minimal, the potential national rewards vast.

This leads to a final point the environmentalists like to ignore: The size of the oilfield that would be developed.

Literature produced by the Sierra Club, Earth First, and other environmental adversaries to the oil and gas industry suggest that oil companies intend to pave most of Alaska with concrete drilling pads. After slogging through the coastal plain bogs and meadows on a Sierra Club tour, *Sierra* associate editor Rauber reported, "we turned to . . . imagining how paving might improve the [wildlife refuge] landscape. This bit could be the BP [British Petroleum] Golf Course, that bluff the Exxon Bar."[10]

It is an amusing conjecture, of course, but superficial and wholly misleading. As starters, the harsh Arctic coastal plain is not only an unlikely, but an impossible locale for a golf course or country club bar. Even if oil companies did plan certain basic amenities for their workers—cafeterias, sleeping quarters, laundries—the fact remains: **the entire area oil companies propose to explore totals about thirteen thousand acres, or roughly 20 square miles.** This represents *less than 1 percent* of the 2,343 square miles in the coastal plain section of the Arctic National Wildlife Refuge, and only about 6/100ths of one percent of the wildlife refuge's 29,296 square miles.

The argument—that the area proposed for development would contaminate the environment of the Arctic National Wildlife Refuge—will simply not stand up under scrutiny. Even if the Arctic National Wildlife Refuge is drilled and found to contain huge pools of oil and gas, at some point drilling will end. Under existing federal and state laws, the land would then be restored (oil and gas companies are required to set aside escrow funds to pay for plugging and abandoning well sites). Gravel pads and roads would be removed, buildings razed, the lands reconstructed, and holding pits emptied and filed with indigenous soil. Within a few years, a visitor would have difficulty determining that drilling activity had ever occurred.

But this is rational, and reason has a hard time pitted against the arguments of environmental extremists, which are an exercise in emotionalism. For example, in his 1992 article in *Sierra*, Rauber said, "Should the plain someday fall into the eager hands of British Petroleum, ARCO and Chevron, there will be 50 to 60 new pools here, wastewater pits with capacities of 13 million gallons each." The image conjured is of huge, filthy black pools of slime and sludge, so full of toxic materials that life forms would be poisoned for all time.

Nonsense.

Maybe there would be fifty to sixty new pools of wastewater, each with a capacity of 13 million gallons each. Or maybe not, because no one knows what would be needed until the actual size of the field is determined. By choosing fifty to sixty as the number, Rauber is tacitly acknowledging that the field is potentially huge. But Rauber failed to report that these would be *temporary* holding tanks to keep the wastewater from contaminating the permafrost or groundwater supplies until it could be cleansed, and then injected into the deep wells. Nor did he report that once the pools were emptied they would be filled with indigenous soil and revegetated in accordance with stringent state and federal regulations.

Ignoring reality seems to be a hallmark of the arguments proposed by extremists in the environmental movement. No one from the Sierra Club or Earth First will discuss the results of restoration at the Kaktovik well site. No fact is allowed to get in the way of a preconceived notion or an antidevelopment sales pitch.

The well-site restoration at the Kaktovik site, where the exploratory seismic well was drilled, showed clearly that environmental recovery could be complete. Within a few years, the appearance of virgin tundra can be assured.

But therein lies the problem. The appearance *of virgin tundra is not sufficient for the more extreme environmentalists. They demand the* fact *of virgin tundra (or forest, or desert, or wherever nature remains untouched). To these purists, the entire North Slope is sacred ground and should not be desecrated by any developmental footprints. This is fundamentally a pious, even sanctimoniously religious response from people who do not hesitate to burn fuel in airplanes to overfly scenic areas, drive in gasoline-powered vehicles to visit national park sites, or eat processed food that requires energy to produce.*

This is an odd contradiction in the environmental movement. To hardcore environmentalists, footsteps apparently do not desecrate the land. But development is strictly taboo. This pseudo-theological explanation— however contradictory—is the only one I have found that fits the intensity of the opposition to opening a minuscule portion of the Arctic National Wildlife Refuge for oil and gas exploration and production.

—DONALD PAUL HODEL

Up to now, and to the nation's detriment, environmentalists have successfully blocked even the most rudimentary efforts to determine the potential energy resources in a fraction on the Arctic National Wildlife Refuge. In late 1991, the Senate refused to consider a bill that would have authorized drilling in less than 0.006 percent of the protected area's almost thirty thousand square miles. The Sierra Club, which had pledged to "draw a line in the tundra," proudly proclaimed:

"The Sierra Club and the environmental movement won a major victory. . . . Senator Bennett Johnston (D-La.), co-author of the energy bill, conceded that 'environmentalists wrote the textbook on how to defeat a bill'. . . . The Arctic Refuge will be at risk until it wins [permanent] wilderness protection. . . ."

This 1991 victory was merely one more in a dismal record of prevention. Throughout the Reagan administration, efforts were made to meet the legitimate environmental objections. The objectives were to allow the most minimal developmental "footprints" for all activities connected with drilling and development, and to guarantee that all developmental projects would be temporary and restorable to their original conditions. Yet every time a proposal went to Capitol Hill,

Congress gave in to the enormous pressure of the environmental organizations, primarily the Sierra Club and Earth First, and blocked any positive actions. In so doing, our nation was sending a message to the world that we did not have the political will even to *look* at what could be the largest oil fields ever discovered in North America. It was like flashing to OPEC a large neon sign that said, "Go ahead and take advantage of us; we're unwilling to help ourselves."

What the environmentalists have not considered is the colossal price that will be paid by the American people if the Arctic National Wildlife Refuge is *not* examined. The down payment will be the destruction of the U.S. oil and gas industry as we know it. And we will see more and more jobs going overseas.

Our energy security has already been dealt with at length, but it cannot be overstressed. If the Arctic coastal plain is not opened up, our dependence on foreign suppliers will certainly jeopardize national security. Already we import about half of the oil consumed each year in the United States.

The argument for energy security also involves the Trans-Alaska Pipeline, whose ecological success story has so embarrassed hard-core environmentalists. But the flow of oil from the Prudhoe Bay field is declining. In 1991, 942.3 million barrels of crude oil were shipped through the Alaska pipeline, down 979.1 million barrels from just two years earlier.[11]

And it is cause for alarm, because at some point in the not-so-distant future, it will become uneconomical to transport oil from Prudhoe Bay to Valdez via the pipeline unless new sources of crude are developed. Development of the Arctic coastal plain would provide just the economic impetus required to keep the Trans-Alaska Pipeline open, and for a sufficient length of time to cultivate new technological recovery methods that can draw even more energy from the Prudhoe Bay field.

Finally, as the experience of Prudhoe Bay and the Kaktovik well site demonstrate, all of this can be accomplished in an environmentally responsible, ecologically sound fashion. It was done at Prudhoe Bay, and it was proved by site restoration of depleted fields in the lower forty-eight states long before tough environmental restrictions were put in place.

In short: The consequences of *not* producing more domestic oil and gas are too serious to be ignored. The crisis in the oil patch is real, and it is immediate.

If we do not develop our enormous oil and gas resources, the economic, political, and social repercussions will echo across the American landscape and the world for generations to come.

CHAPTER SIX

THE WAGES OF IMPRUDENCE

PART I

THE ECONOMIC COST OF KILLING A BASIC INDUSTRY

Michel Halbouty is one of the petroleum industry's Grand Old Men. Born in 1909, he has been actively engaged in punching holes in the ground to look for oil and gas since 1930 when he graduated from Texas A&M University with a degree in geological petroleum engineering. (He acquired a master's degree in 1931, and another in 1955.)

A brash, flinty octogenarian whose directness reflects the grit necessary to survive and prosper over sixty years in a tough industry, Halbouty says the crisis in the oil patch isn't impending; it is already here. High taxes, unnecessary environmental restraints, excessive regulation, and public policies that encourage consumption of foreign oil have combined to place the U.S. oil and gas industry at the top of the list of economically endangered species.

"The industry today is dying," Halbouty says. "By 1995 it will be gone. The independents will be dead. And when that happens you're going to see gas lines that are measured in miles, not blocks."

* * *

For many Americans who disdain property rights, it is easy to dismiss the perilous state of the U.S. oil and gas business. After all, the argument runs, no sympathy should accrue to wealthy investors who speculate in nature's bountiful resources for their own private gain without returning any of their profits to the socio-economic system that sustains them.

If the current crisis in the oil patch were only a matter of wealthy oil investors savaging the environment to get richer, it could be resolved without a great deal of political difficulty. The most obvious actions would be a repeat of what we have already seen: a punitive tax to prevent unreasonable profits coupled with severe environmental regulatory measures.

But the fact is that the nation's oil and gas explorers and producers do return much of what they earn to the people they serve. This return is made in tax payments, environmental clean-up and antipollution expenditures, and myriad other ways.

Yet the general populace has not even a rudimentary understanding of what oil wildcatters—independents who drill for oil in unproven fields, with at best a 30 percent chance of finding it and more commonly a 10 percent success ratio—do or why they do it. This is true even though the business is not particularly complicated. The oil and gas industry operates like any other capitalistic enterprise: you try to find oil for a lower cost than you receive for selling it.

But the equation becomes confused when public-policy elements are introduced to control both buying and selling. For example, until the windfall profits tax was removed, oil and gas producers had to determine *when* their energy was discovered, and at what finding price. Taxes were then levied to control the difference between that price and what oil was selling for on the open market. This became complicated because a determination had to be made about where the sale occurred—the New York Commodities Exchange, or some other market. Finally, the producer, in order to compute his or her taxes, had to calculate the prevailing price on a given date. All of this can drive accountants crazy, because the posted market price of oil today— the price quoted in newspapers—has been set by a commodity futures market in New York City that often is regulated more by gambling instincts among traders than by any rational market equilibrium between buyers and sellers. For proof, review how the oil futures market reacted in 1990 when Saddam Hussein invaded Kuwait. The price of oil shot skyward—traders' fear of a shortage—despite a worldwide surplus of oil. Within hours, oil prices dipped back to previous levels that reflected real supply and demand balances.

The result has often been a sharp difference between quoted market prices for crude oil and refined products and what consumers actually pay at the gas pump and for heating oil.[1] But as we have seen in a previous chapter, the industry has not explained itself adequately and has thus become a convenient scapegoat whenever fuel prices rise and consumers feel a pinch.

Over the years the Opinion Research Corp. has tracked public sentiment toward the oil and gas industry. A graphic representation of the results since 1975 clearly shows how public sentiment toward the industry rises and falls with gasoline prices. In 1965, for example, almost 80 percent of the adults surveyed by ORC had a "favorable" image of the oil and gas industry, while less than 10 percent viewed the industry in an "unfavorable light." By 1975, after the gas lines and rising prices following the Arab oil embargo in 1973, the "favorable" category dropped to about 22 percent, while an "unfavorable" image of the oil and gas industry rose to more than 40 percent. It got worse after Iran started withholding oil from the world market in 1979 and prices shot even higher. That year, the "unfavorable" respondents totaled 60 percent, with fewer than 20 percent of those polled having a "favorable" image.

Obviously, consumer prices influence public opinion, especially when accompanied by political distortions and superficial media reporting. There's no question that the U.S. oil and gas industry gets blamed whenever consumer prices rise, even when the reason for the price hikes are beyond the industry's control, as they were in 1973 and 1979.

Whenever the oil and gas industry is involved in public policy debate, some politicians, TV commentators, and many mass-media writers dismiss reason in favor of emotional arguments that grab the attention. Their argument goes this way:

Great wealth is wrong in a society anchored at the bottom by people who live in poverty. People who are wealthy are evil in degrees that vary according to the size of their bank accounts. The more money you have, the more evil you must be. Policy analyst Richard B. McKenzie of the Center for the Study of American Business at Washington University in St. Louis observed in a 1992 article, "The energy-policy debate has often been framed by the media, and by competing political interests, as a conflict between the forces of 'good' and 'evil.' "[2]

With the contestants of the battle thus irrationally defined, who are the worst people of all? To the media and populist politicians, the answer is easy: the lowest are the people who make money by providing the commodities that we all must have in order to live, that is, our "necessities." Under this thesis it is perfectly fine to make a fortune by peddling hula hoops, pet rocks, rap records, violent videotapes, or by hitting a baseball or anchoring the evening news—that is, doing something or making something the public will buy but really does not need and can survive without. But it is not acceptable to amass riches by providing capital to develop and sell commodities people must have to live and maintain a decent standard of existence.

Many of these basic commodities are furnished by extractive industries: oil and gas that fuel our cars, pickups, and homes; coal that generates electrical power; timber that is used to construct our houses, apartments, offices, and factories; rock and gravel that make cement for our roads and bridges, and so on.

And these extractive industries also take those basic commodities from an environment that is the legacy of every human being born and unborn. Thus the person who becomes wealthy by selling basic commodities is branded by a stain of guilt that is more tainted than that imposed on other "capitalists"—a word used pejoratively by many people.

Unfortunately, the issue is not this simple. It is not a conflict between "good" and "evil." Much more is at work than political rhetoric about penalizing rich people or protecting the environment, however much some political leaders would have us believe it to be so.

And that is because, without exaggeration, the survival of our domestic oil and gas industry is essential to the survival of the nation and our standard of living. The domestic energy industry is as important to our existence as the grain planted and reaped by an Iowa farmer, the beef produced by Western cattle ranchers, the milk that flows from the dairies of Wisconsin and the Upper Midwest. Even farming has become an energy-intensive industry, as Btus (British thermal units, a standard of energy measurement) have replaced human labor.

Moreover, the people whose lives will be most directly affected by any crisis in the oil patch are hardly wealthy. The people most harmed will be those at the lower end of the socio-economic ladder. Poor people will feel the pain more than any other single group because the economic principles that govern the oil and gas industry are based upon consumer necessity, not choice. Petroleum products and the industries driven by oil and gas are not optional to most people, except perhaps for a handful of hermits. The oil and gas industry's mechanism begins in this elementary way:

More Oil and Gas = Lower energy costs.

Lower Energy Costs = Lower prices for all energy-based products—virtually every commodity or service we need for modern life, especially food, clothing, shelter, heating, and transportation.

The question is: who benefits the most from abundant energy and low oil and gas prices? Is it the wealthy, most particularly the rich investors in the oil and gas industry? Or is it the middle class and people grasping the lower rungs of the economic ladder?

Obviously, it is the people at the bottom of the ladder. The less money poor or middle-class people are required to spend on energy and on goods and services heavily dependent on energy, the more money they will have for other basic needs such as health care, education, insurance, and so on.

Consider for a moment the reverse equation, assuming a constant level of demand for energy products:

Less Oil and Gas = Higher energy costs.

Higher Energy Costs = Higher prices for all energy-based products—virtually every commodity or service needed for modern life, especially food, clothing, shelter, heating, and transportation.

Clearly this is going to make it more difficult for lower-income people to survive. Just as clearly, higher energy costs are not so important to wealthy people. The wealthy have sufficient resources to live in relative comfort regardless of an upward drift in energy prices.

Some will argue that this brief analysis has a flaw, that the economic laws of supply and demand usually dictate that the demand curve begins to fall away as prices rise. This means poor people will do without, or find alternative products to supply their needs, no matter how much they might suffer. And, in the circumstances that prevailed before the huge oilfields of the Middle East were discovered this might have been true. After all, the nation learned to live with all sorts of rationed products, energy included, during World War II.

But it is no longer true. Until well after World War II, the United States supplied most of its own oil and gas. But since 1980, as we have seen, while overall demand has remained relatively constant the nature of the supply curve has dramatically shifted. The overall consumption trend has not been altered, and U.S. supplies have been fairly steady except for temporary blips up or down. But the *components* of supply have been significantly refashioned. The first hints of this change came in the 1973 embargo, when U.S. oil imports actually increased despite reduced supplies from the Middle East. This apparent contradiction was due to a federal policy: the government chose to punish the domestic oil and gas industry rather than OPEC for rising fuel prices.

And thus, where once most of our oil and gas came from domestic supplies, today it is mostly imported. In 1950, the U.S. imported only about 13 percent of the oil used; by 1960, the figure had risen to a modest 20 percent. After OPEC lifted its 1973 oil embargo, it rose sharply to almost 50 percent. This was followed by a downward trend in the middle 1980s to a low of slightly above 30 percent, which reflected both increased domestic production and reduced demand because of higher prices.

But then the full impact of new environmental regulations and tax laws began to be felt. Independent oil and gas producers dropped out by the thousands, and imports began to climb steeply.

By the summer of 1992, for the first time in history, the nation imported more oil than it produced. The magic halfway line was crossed in July 1992; 52 percent of the oil we consumed that month was imported—about 8 million barrels a day, or a total of almost 250 million barrels for the month. Despite the ominous implications of this trend, American consumers remain addicted to oil—for the simple reason that oil is cheaper and more convenient than alternative energy supplies.

This has profound economic implications for every American. It is one of the variants that make the customary economic equations invalid. And for several reasons. A major one is that we are making domestic oil more expensive through environmental regulation. This is national policy. But we do not—and cannot—impose the same environmental regulations on the oil we import from overseas. We could, of course, attach an environmental fee that would reflect foreign environmental responsibility. This would be one step toward leveling the playing field. But it would hardly be sufficient and might even violate at least the spirit of the General Agreement on Tariffs and Trade (GATT) treaty that regulates international trade.

Clearly, if the trend of reliance on unreliable supplies of foreign oil continues, and it almost surely will without a renewed vitality in the U.S. oil and gas industry, the economic consequences are predictable and frightening. Some of those possibilities—probabilities, one might safely suggest—need to be examined.

The first scenario envisions no change in demand for petroleum products, no new or relaxed tax laws, continued environmental policies that restrict domestic drilling, and a stable international political climate that could guarantee a steady supply of foreign oil. In other words, we continue to get cheap oil. Since the source of supply will not matter, we will rely more and more each year on foreign suppliers because it will continue to be cheaper to pump petroleum from overseas fields than in the United States.

In these circumstances, it can reasonably be argued (as Michel Halbouty does) that the already severely crippled independent sector of U.S. oil and gas producers will be destroyed for all practical purposes within the next decade.

But therein lies the problem, because independent explorers historically have found about 80 percent of all new oil fields in the United States. Over the past decade, the number of independents has fallen by almost two-thirds, and the dropout rate can be expected to accelerate. In fact, most independent producers today have simply stopped looking for new oil. Instead, they are either pumping from existing fields or buying production sites from major oil companies, which are themselves abandoning U.S. wells in favor of cheaper overseas investments.

As two prominent oil industry executives told the U.S. Senate's Finance Committee and Joint Committee on taxation in a March 1990 briefing:

"U.S. extraction investments are not competitive with foreign . . . investments at virtually every price level and level of geological risk." This is because cash generated by an "average" U.S. prospect well yields "negative present values to investors after all financial claims on U.S. oil and gas production are taken out . . . despite the fact that these same prospects add significant economic wealth to U.S. society in general and positive revenue gains to both federal and state treasuries."[3] In layman's language this means that, thanks largely to federal and state taxes, an investor is likely to lose money on every barrel of oil pumped from an average domestic well.

The result? Continuing increases in oil imports, even if the Clinton administration's efforts (whose weaknesses are discussed in chapter 9) to reduce demand are 100 percent effective. And this is because our domestic production will continue to shrink, and probably at a faster rate than any decline in demand. In the unlikely short-term prospect that there is a corresponding decline in demand, our reliance on foreign oil will still grow at a faster rate than the American Petroleum Institute's current projection of about 1 percentage point per year because domestic production is falling. It is irrelevant whether this foreign oil is produced by a U.S.-based company such as Exxon, Mobil, or Chevron, or by a state-owned company in Saudi Arabia, Kuwait, or Iran. The oil will originate overseas and not from domestic fields.

Even if foreign supplies were as predictable as tomorrow's sunrise, two compelling economic reasons exist to rebut the proposition that the geographic source of our energy is irrelevant.

The first is the impact on employment in the United States. A continued decline in domestic oil-patch jobs will mean exporting more pay checks, technical drilling and production expertise, and investments in technology and equipment. This will have a severe impact not only on the U.S. petroleum industry, but on the industries that service and supply it.

In turn, this will produce a geometric, not parallel, decline in economic wealth flowing to U.S. individuals (lost jobs), fewer goods and services supplied to the oil and gas industry by U.S. businesses, and a decline in tax revenues to federal, state, and local governments (from lost income taxes on paychecks and corporate profits, and reduced severance, production, and ad valorem taxes). These, combined, will have a decided negative economic effect.

The second reason why we should reduce our reliance on foreign oil can be found in the nation's alarming trade gap numbers. The United States has not enjoyed a favorable balance of trade since 1975, when we exported $8.9 billion more goods and services than we imported. Since then, the trade gap has yawned to a high of almost $160 billion in 1987. In 1992, the trade gap totaled $84.5 billion. (And, significantly, almost 53 percent—$44.5 billion in all—was attributable to petroleum imports.)

The significance of a negative balance of payments is that it withdraws domestic wealth that otherwise could be used for investment in job-producing activities such as capital improvements and research and development. Our trade gap has gotten so out of kilter that, today, most economists talk about how to reduce the gap rather than how to close it.

This is where oil fits into the picture. *Our purchases of foreign oil have contributed more to the growth of the trade deficit than any other single commodity.* In fact, over the past twenty-plus years we have imported more oil than the net difference between our purchases and sales of automobiles, electronics equipment, and other finished goods. In the twenty-two-year period from 1970 to 1992, petroleum imports have totaled $924.5 billion.

This is *more than 73 percent* of the cumulative trade gap of $1.26 trillion during that twenty-one-year period.[4]

Oil imports are usually either the largest or second-largest single commodity to pass into the United States through customs in any given year. In 1990, for example, petroleum and related products accounted for more than 12 percent of the $495.3 billion we spent on all commodities produced overseas. The approximately $50 billion spent on foreign oil[5] for domestic consumption was exceeded that year only by the $73 billion worth of cars and trucks imported mostly from Canada, Japan, and Western Europe. (It should be noted that this sum was offset by $31 billion in U.S.-made vehicles exported, for a negative trade imbalance in the automotive sector of $42 billion, or less than our negative cost for importing oil.) (See Figure 6.1.)

We are currently importing about $1 billion worth of oil each week,

Figure 6.1
PETROLEUM'S CONTRIBUTION TO THE U.S. TRADE DEFICIT
1980 – 1991
(Dollars in billions)

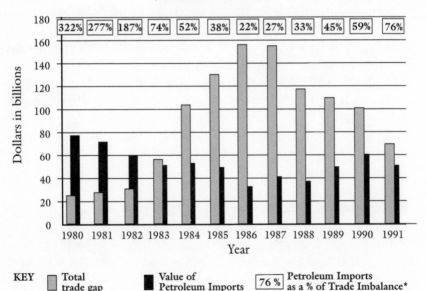

KEY ▢ Total trade gap   ■ Value of Petroleum Imports   76 % Petroleum Imports as a % of Trade Imbalance*

12-Year Totals $ 929.6 billion $ 644.5 billion   69%

*Rounded to nearest whole number.

SOURCE: Statistical Abstract of the United States 1992, Table 1330, p. 796.

$142.9 million each day, almost $6 million, about 300,000 barrels, every hour of every day of the year. If our imports could be replaced by domestic production to offset even a third of the trade imbalance, the result would be more jobs for our economy than the entire $16 billion "job-creation" legislation proposed by President Clinton. And these productive jobs would enrich the entire economic structure; they would not be make-work employment intended only to lower unemployment statistics.

And, as suggested earlier, the trade imbalance also has an impact on the size of the ballooning federal deficit, which almost everybody agrees is the nation's most immediate economic and political dilemma. This is not a matter of comparing apples and oranges. Because while these are different economic data-bases, one (the trade gap) influences the other (federal tax receipts). When private-sector wealth flows overseas, that money cannot be invested in the United States. This means less wealth is produced and absorbed within our own borders, which, among other things, reduces our job base, which reduces the tax base.

And with the domestic oil and gas industry, the trade-gap/budget imbalance gets a double-whammy. The first blow is delivered by importing about $50 billion worth of oil each year and having that money flow overseas rather than into the U.S. economic infrastructure. The second comes as the domestic energy industry shrinks and U.S. jobs and capital flow overseas to the Middle East, Pacific Rim, North Sea, and other major foreign oil-producing locations.

The scenario described above is happening now. It is, in effect, the first equation, as already described. To repeat:

Ample energy available at low prices provides reasonable prices on all fuels and also benefits the basic goods and services industries heavily dependent on energy. It works most favorably for the lower- and middle-income members of the population, since they benefit the most from inexpensive oil and gas.

The problem, though, is that half of the cheaply produced energy Americans enjoy today is coming from foreign fields. Unless something happens to change current trends, it is entirely possible that by the year 2000 we will be importing 70-plus percent of our oil.

What would happen if foreign oil supplies were suddenly interrupted?

This is a nightmare, true, but one with very high possibilities. Indeed, it has happened twice in the past twenty years; two-and-a-half times, if you add Saddam Hussein's attempt to take over the Kuwaiti fields in 1990. These shortages did not occur because oil was unavailable. On the contrary, in each case worldwide oil supplies were abundant. But also in each case foreign energy producers made conscious political decisions to turn off the oil spigot to pursue goals that had nothing to do with the oil market or energy supply and demand.

A similar threat still exists. Most of the world's major oil producing nations, excluding the United States, are politically unstable, politically fragile, and militarily vulnerable. Look at Saudi Arabia, for example. It owns the world's largest oil reserves—in 1990, it claimed nearly 260 billion barrels of proven oil beneath its soil and offshore waters. And, as you may recall, Saudi Arabia was a leader in cutting off the flow of oil to the U.S. in 1973. While the Saudis were our allies in Desert Storm, they remain a dedicated Moslem nation, hostile to secularism, wary of Israeli influence, and suspicious of U.S. intentions. Indeed, the United States, as well as any other country, is guided by the same principles that governed British foreign policy during the empire's halcyon years of the late nineteenth century: "No lasting friends, no lasting enemies, only lasting interests." The same can be said of Saudi Arabia, as well.

Saudi Arabia's only real national asset is its huge oil inventories.[6] The nation's petroleum reserves represent a mammoth bargaining chip at the poker table of international petropolitics. The same can be said of the Kuwaitis, who still have oil reserves approaching 100 billion barrels. Iraq and Iran are also major players, each with some 100 billion barrels of proven oil reserves, despite the burnoff of almost 100 million barrels when Saddam Hussein torched the Kuwaiti fields. Is it wise to place our energy destiny in the hands of Saudi Arabia, Iraq, Kuwait, or Iran? There are, of course, differences among them.

The Saudis, like Iran and Iraq, are fundamentally religious and hostile to Israel. But unlike Iran and Iraq, the Saudis tend to be trustworthy provided one understands the imperatives they face. Saudi Arabia has a relatively small population (under 10 million people), compared with their neighboring militant powers, Iran and Iraq (populations about 60 million and 20 million, respectively, by 1991 estimates). The holiest of all Moslem mosques are in Mecca and Medina, both in Saudi Arabia, and are held "in trust" for the entire Moslem world. The Saudi kingdom could not long survive if it were deemed disloyal to the principles of Mohammed by the Moslem world.

The Saudis are also well aware of their own reliance on oil, having no other economic resources. They know the sensitivity of the market to changes in price and availability of oil. These they regard as opportunities for the furtherance of their national interest. To say that the Saudis are trustworthy means that they can be trusted to pursue their own national interest—and not ours, unless these interests coincide as they did in Desert Shield and Desert Storm.

Even less reliable than the Middle Eastern oil producers are the Russians, despite and partly because of the fall of communism. The former Soviet states are probably more unstable than any other modern society at this time. Eastern Europe has settled into an unfamiliar but working accommodation with democratic political institutions and free-market economics. But the former Soviet Union has not yet been able to achieve this stability. This poses a problem since Russia is one of the world's largest potential oil suppliers. At the end of 1990, the former USSR had almost 60 billion barrels of proven oil reserves, more than twice that of the United States and exceeded only by Venezuela and, among the OPEC nations, by Saudi Arabia, Kuwait, Iraq, Iran, and the United Arab Emirates.

The chances of an interruption of Russian oil supplies are great. This is important not so much in respect to what the Russians now export, which is negligible, but what they could supply in the event OPEC production is disrupted. The Russians, however, are having trouble meeting their own domestic and former satellites' oil needs. Their problem is not so much international politics, like the Saudis', as it is an internal stability that continues to be elusive. Their understanding and interpretation of democratic processes and free-market economic mechanisms are at best hazy.

We cannot, in short, count on any foreign nation, even our traditional friends, such as Great Britain (only recently a net exporter of oil, after major finds in the North Sea), much less our reluctant and occasional allies in the OPEC cartel and the former Soviet Union.

And so, back to the question: What if a major portion of those oil supplies were suddenly cut off?

First, what would a "major" interruption be? If it were 1 million barrels a day—about 16 percent of our present import consumption—our Strategic Petroleum Reserve could make up the shortfall, at least for a while. Even so, oil prices would rise, as would inflation. If the reduction were 3 million barrels per day—or almost half of our import needs—and lasted longer than three months, the nation would be in a world of hurt. In the first place, only about 2 million barrels a day can be pumped from the Strategic Petroleum Reserve. Not only this, but the Strategic Petroleum Reserve could provide enough oil supply to meet current domestic demand for only seven to eight months. And that is true only if you assume no political miscalculations in utilizing the Strategic Petroleum Reserve—an assumption of almost heroic proportions. Moreover, very substantial price increases for fuel and fuel-based goods and services would occur. Transportation would be dislocated. And industries would shut down or curtail production. Domestic production might increase, but it would take time for the industry to gear up to meet supply shortages.

In any event, even a brief, three-month dislocation of oil imports would make the price of U.S. petroleum products skyrocket overnight. In each of the two recent experiences, the dislocation was temporary. But what if the chokehold were of a more permanent nature?

For openers lower-income and middle-class consumers would find their lifestyles altered almost as quickly as oil prices zoomed skyward. This would have nothing to do with oil companies "gouging people to make obscene profits." It would be a simple matter of economic supply and demand: oil companies would have to replace current low-cost inventories with higher-priced, less-available foreign oil. Either that, or buy oil and gas domestically. Which would be impossible in the amounts required, since domestic oil and gas producers are being driven overseas.

Consequently, consumers would be required to pay more for energy and voluntarily ration their fuel expenditures. People would drive less, buy more fuel-efficient vehicles, and pay a higher price for doing so. They would pay more for virtually all foods they consume, as well as for electricity and heating oil or natural gas.

All of this would have a dramatic impact on inflation, which would go on an upward rampage. Increased prices would not be confined to transportation, but would touch food, plastics, fibers—the list is almost endless.[7] Dollars would be worth quarters, quarters nickels, and nickels pennies. The 1970s and early 1980s are good examples of how escalating energy prices sparked an inflationary spiral in almost every consumer commodity. And at that time, our reliance on overseas oil supplies was not nearly so great as it is today.

Furthermore, if the past is a guide, government would get in on the act, establishing mandatory fuel-usage standards for everything from cars and speed limits to home thermostat settings. New bureaucracies would be established to spend huge sums of money to develop alternative energy sources, resulting in even more deficit spending than ever.

In short, the nation would be forced into an unwelcome pattern of tougher, lower standards of living. Inflation would be on an upswing, and people's savings would be eroded. Interest rates almost surely would rise, costing businesses more to invest in new plant and equipment as their energy-based operating expenses spiraled upward. This would result in massive layoffs and choke off new job growth. Tax revenues would decline at the very moment new revenues would be required to retrain jobless workers and to provide food stamps and make welfare payments.

Equally bad, an interruption of foreign oil supplies would affect United States exports because most of the goods we send overseas cannot be produced without energy.

For example, take agricultural products. You cannot farm without fuel, and not just the diesel fuels that power the tractors that till the land. Beyond this, oil and gas are fundamental to manufacturing the fertilizers that make the soil productive. Other than the money invested in the land, energy is the largest or second-largest single cost component of growing wheat, corn, pork, beef cattle, and other agricultural products. What's more, all agricultural products must be transported to processing or marketing facilities, and these costs would also rise along with gasoline and diesel-fuel prices.

This is what makes U.S. energy supplies essential not only to the United States, but to the rest of the world as well. In 1991 the United States exported $36.1 billion worth of agricultural products, up more than 50 percent from $23.8 billion only five years earlier. The heartland of the United States, the Midwestern plains that shimmer in endless fields of wheat and corn, soybeans and other grains, is wholly dependent upon energy. Without energy, hundreds of thousands of acres of rich agricultural land would lie fallow, awaiting not seeds that could germinate and grow food but energy that could grow that food on a scale sufficient to feed the United States and other nations as well. Not inconceivably, the United States might not be much better off than Russia, where presently desperately needed food rots because the transportation system cannot get it to market.

The questions occur: Wouldn't it be possible to increase domestic oil and gas production quickly to compensate for a loss of foreign imports? Or couldn't we shift speedily to alternative energy supplies?

The quick answer is easy: No.

The domestic oil and gas industry in the United States has already sustained damage that cannot be repaired in the short run. Too many jobs have been lost or exported overseas, too much equipment has been idled for too long—it is rusting and cannot be put back to work quickly.

It would be impossible to find enough skilled workers in two or three months to return industry employment to the 2 million level of the early 1980s era, when domestic producers supplied more than 60 percent of our consumption demand. And many of the four thousand rigs used a decade ago have been cannibalized for spare parts, dismantled for salvage, or otherwise abandoned. Granted that the Kuwaiti crisis demonstrated a remarkable resilience in developing domestic supplies. But each time the domestic industry is required to rebound because of an interruption of foreign supplies, the length of time that comeback requires gets longer.

Nor could alternative sources be developed quickly enough to satisfy a continued level of demand. Construction of nuclear generating plants takes years, decades, in some cases. Squeezing oil from shale requires billions of dollars in capital investment, and years to construct the manufacturing facilities required for the process. Alternative fuels are not a short-term answer.

Our increasing reliance on foreign oil supplies and the withering of our domestic energy industry are dangerous economic facts. In allowing the situation to take place, we have ignored both history and the harsh, complex realities of modern economics and geopolitics. It is still not too late to turn the long-term situation around, however hazardous the short-range situation might be. But time is running out.

CHAPTER SEVEN

THE WAGES OF IMPRUDENCE
PART II

THE POLITICAL COST OF KILLING
A BASIC INDUSTRY

Steve Allen is the consummate All-American young man. A darkly handsome, thirty-one-year-old six-footer, he's married and the father of a pixieish preschool daughter. Steve Allen attends church regularly and is almost reverent in his belief in the American system of government and free-market economics.

For most of his adult life, Steve Allen worked in the Oklahoma oil patch. But today, he is an appraiser for the Seminole County, Oklahoma, tax assessor and earns about $750 a month—about half (less, given inflation) the $1,500 a month he was getting in the early 1980s when he was working on a drilling rig in the Anadarko Basin at the height of the energy boom. In fact, if you count the medical, housing, and food benefits, the $750 Steve Allen earns today is less than he was paid as a sergeant in the Oklahoma National Guard when he was called to duty with the 101st Airborne in 1990 and sent to the Arabian Peninsula during Desert Shield and Desert Storm. In the Gulf War, Steve Allen served as a computer supply specialist, arranging for advanced depots to supply the airborne troopers with clothing, food, fuel, and ammunition. It was

107

tough, dangerous duty, often requiring him to go to an advanced position to set up a supply base before the combat troops arrived. But since Steve Allen is a patriot, he was proud to serve his country.

When he returned in the summer of 1991, he found that there were no jobs in Oklahoma for out-of-work oilfield roustabouts. As in the rest of the oil patch, the industry in Oklahoma was shrinking, and with it employment possibilities. Between the beginning of 1990 and the end of 1991, the number of oil and gas extraction jobs in Oklahoma declined by 2,500, to 37,900 from 40,400—almost 7 percent of all petroleum exploration and production jobs in the state. Steve Allen had to leave the oil and gas industry and take a lower-paying job to feed his family. But his $750 salary as a tax assessor was insufficient to cover car payments, and he had to sell his pickup truck.

Steve Allen is not just a human statistic. He is a very real human caught painfully in a contradictory, even cruel national policy. This policy panders to consumers' demands for cheap energy by importing "inexpensive" foreign oil; at the same time, it allows a domestic industry to be rocked by punitive taxes and regulatory restraints. This perverse policy, in effect, encourages foreign energy development and foreign jobs at the expense of a domestic industry and its workers. The question leaps out:

Where is the economic sense or moral justice in a national policy that sends young American men and women to risk their lives to secure a continuing supply of cheap Middle Eastern oil, while pursuing a political course at home that clamps down on cheap energy at home and denies these men and women employment in an essential industry of their choice?

The answer is easy for Steve Allen: "It doesn't make you feel very good about your own country. I don't know what to think about my country. It's confusing."

Oil drives not only the machinery of transportation, commerce, and industry. It also propels U.S. political policies both nationally and internationally. The two are inextricably linked. Begin with domestic politics.

The political domestic discord over oil and gas exploration and production is basically an interstate, or regional, rivalry. Oil-rich states such as Texas, Oklahoma, Louisiana, and Alaska generally want a national energy policy that encourages domestic drilling and production, which would boost their tax bases and bring them prosperity.

This usually, but not always, involves supporting tax structures that encourage the industry as well as environmental health and safety regulations that are not unreasonably harsh. Citizens of energy-rich states tend to be in favor of higher petroleum prices nationwide, because higher prices mean jobs and income. Their own energy needs can be filled at more modest prices because they have abundant energy available and their transportation costs are lower.

In contrast, regions with little or no oil and gas production, such as most of the Eastern Seaboard states from New England to Florida, want cheap fuel for their automobiles and homes. (This is not to say that these regions don't possess oil and gas deposits. They do. But for various reasons, primarily vocal opposition from environmental groups, these fields generally have not been explored.) In addition, these states tend to be more environmentally extreme than the major oil-producing states (with the obvious exception of California). One reason these states can enjoy the luxury of "righteousness" is because the burden of environmental costs does not fall as heavily on states that do not produce oil and gas, at least openly; they are not directly paying a price in lost jobs, reduced tax bases, or production revenues that drive an oil-based regional economy. This fantasy can be maintained for as long as the non-energy producing states have ample supplies of reasonably inexpensive fuel. They do not realize that they are unnecessarily paying a higher price for the energy they consume.

The problem with this posture, which is encouraged by these states' politicians, is that it is phony, not based on facts. And these facts are: First, drilling for oil and gas can be done safely, without damage to the environment, and production can be achieved without treading on environmental toes. This has been proven time and again. But the politically correct viewpoint is to deny these demonstrated facts—an attitude that is massaged by the media amidst loud proclamations of fairness and objectivity. Second, we all pay for environmental health and safety standards imposed on the oil and gas industry, regardless of where the energy is produced, or who produces it.

In short, oil-poor states want controls and regulatory structures and at least a short-term flow of relatively cheap energy, whether it comes from overseas or from the United States. It is a short-sighted view, but understandable.

This regional rivalry has burst out every time petroleum shortages have occurred. In the late 1970s and early 1980s, when the Iranians withheld oil, creating a fuel famine, one of the most popular songs in Texas, Oklahoma, and Louisiana was titled, "Freeze a Yankee." The song's central theme was that the oil-rich Southwestern United States should not have to endure long gas lines at a time when Texas was shipping huge quantities of home-heating oil and natural gas to New England.

Nor have oil-poor states been any more charitable toward the Southwest. In March 1993, for example, a delegation of New England members of Congress urged that home-heating oil, which is a primary residential fuel in the Northeastern United States, be exempted from President Clinton's proposed new taxes on energy (which, of course, ultimately failed in the form originally proposed). These energy-poor states were granted a year's delay in paying the Clinton administration's proposed Btu tax on home-heating fuel, never mind that this exemption was clearly discriminatory.

These members of Congress were unable to explain (nor, to be fair, did they have any obligation to do so) how it was equitable for New Englanders to continue having cheap, untaxed home-heating fuel, while the West, where more driving miles are logged because of the vast distances, was being hit hard by increased gasoline taxes. But, then, fairness is not wedded to politics. Nor is fairness an issue in this regional rivalry. The issue is economic self-interest.

What these conflicting arguments ignore, however, is that where long-term, adequate supplies of energy are involved, self-interest ought to be measured by national, not state or regional objectives. Our current crisis in the oil patch affects the entire nation, not just oil-poor New England or the oil-rich Southwest. Logically, the entire nation and all its regions benefit from federal incentives to invest in exploration and development of domestic oil and gas. The increased supply keeps prices at reasonable levels. The increased investment finds oil and gas and creates jobs in the oil-producing states. It can be a win-win situation rather than a lose-lose one.

Logic notwithstanding, Congress continues to look at energy policies as a regional dispute rather than as a problem that needs to be considered from a national—indeed, an international—viewpoint. In a narrow context, the forces that argue for "cheap foreign oil" have dominated. Several factors have combined in this political debate to favor the non-oil producing states.

One of these factors, as noted in chapter 4, is the politically potent environmental movement, which has been manipulated by a radical leadership over the past twenty years. Their objective, quite simply, is to stop all hydrocarbon energy usage. That cannot be accomplished, of course, without either a cataclysmic impact on our economy or a truly monumental breakthrough in the means of energy production and use. Something over 40 percent of our overall national energy and more than 99 percent of our transportation energy needs come from crude petroleum products.

But since our demands for cheap energy can—at least at present—be fulfilled through oil imports, the environmentalists have been able to persuade Congress and state legislators to impose costly environmental regulations on the domestic oil and gas industry, never mind the destructive cumulative effect. Consider these numbers:

According to the American Petroleum Institute, in 1992 the U.S. oil and gas industry spent $8 billion on environmental costs necessary to explore and produce oil and gas domestically. This was almost as much as the $8.6 billion the industry spent on actual exploration and production drilling, and more than five times the $1.5 billion spent to acquire new properties thought to contain undiscovered oil and gas. And this is only the beginning. Over the next twenty years, environmental proposals to regulate oil and gas exploration, production, and transportation, *proposals already approved by Congress*, will cost the industry an additional $9.8 billion every year, and perhaps as much as three times that amount, or $27.8 billion. That's right—the $27.8 billion figure is an estimate of annual, not cumulative, expenditures. Obviously, no weakened industry can absorb such a pummeling for long without even more brutal cutbacks in production, or simply conceding defeat and going out of business.

Another factor, mentioned previously, that has worked to the disadvantage of oil and gas producers is the industry's inability or unwillingness to gain public support for and understanding of the mechanisms that influence oil and gas economics. Before the spread of consumer and environmental movements, perhaps it made sense for producers to focus their public relations efforts on individual legislators. But that is no longer true. Today, public opinion—inflamed by media disinformation—has a far more powerful influence on politics than a relatively small group of pro-oil politicians.

The wild card that politicians of both parties have been able to play in this high-stakes game—one that has made it easier for energy-poor states to exercise political dominance over the energy-rich—has been the abundance of overseas petroleum supplies. Oil-rich nations such as Mexico, Venezuela, Saudi Arabia, Kuwait, Iran, Iraq, the United Arab Emirates, Indonesia, and others, have been able to satisfy America's voracious appetite for oil and gas and at a relatively low price of about $20 a barrel on average in recent years.

Mexico and Venezuela are good examples. Mexico's gross domestic product rose by 64 percent between 1980 and 1990. During this period Mexican crude-oil exports to the United States rose by almost 50 percent, to 276.9 million barrels in 1990 from 185.5 million barrels ten years earlier. Venezuela provides an even more impressive statistical linkage between oil exports and its domestic wealth. Between 1980 and 1990, Venezuela's gross domestic product increased by 42 percent; its exports of crude oil rose by almost 330 percent, to 244 million barrels in 1990 from 57 million barrels in 1980.

This partly explains how and why world oil reserves have grown so dramatically over the past three decades. With a ravenous market in the United States—and, latterly, in many other parts of the world—developing nations were encouraged to look for oil, most often with outside help from U.S. exploration and production companies. A surprising number of those nations found oil in impressive quantities. In 1960, for example, only one nation in the Pacific Rim, Indonesia, had measurable oil reserves of more than 1 billion barrels. Today, a total of 18.6 billion barrels of proven reserves have been found beneath Australia, Brunei, India, Malaysia, and Indonesia. (In the latter, reserves have dropped by almost 3 billion barrels, to 6.6 billion barrels at the end of 1992.)

Another measurement: In 1960, the world's total proven reserves were 302 billion barrels, of which the United States' 33.5 billion barrels represented slightly more than 11 percent. By 1992, world oil reserves had more than tripled to 991 billion barrels, while U.S. reserves had fallen almost 22 percent to 26.3 billion barrels, which had become less than 3 percent of the world's total. What these numbers demonstrate is that it has become more economical to look for oil overseas than in the United States. Domestic oil has become more expensive because unrealistic and artificial restraints on U.S. oil production have made it so.

The result was inevitable: Over the years spanning the 1970s and 1980s, U.S. imports of crude oil began inching upward. In 1970, the United States imported 21 percent of its oil. Between 1974 and 1980, the ratio of imports to usage rose an average of 40.6 percent each year, largely because of higher imports from non-OPEC nations to replace oil lost to the 1973 OPEC embargo and Iran's shutdown of exports to the United States in 1979.

By 1985, however, imports had settled back to a much more comfortable 26 percent of domestic consumption. The primary reasons for this were increased activity in the U.S. oil industry and reduced consumption. When oil prices were in the high $30 per barrel range, with expectations that they might rise to $40 a barrel or more, independent producers were spurred to look for new oil and gas reserves. And, once drilling was financed and had begun, it made sense to continue work even if the anticipated price hikes did not materialize. Of course, once a well was brought in, it could produce oil at a positive cash flow at even $10 a barrel as long as the sales price exceeded production costs.

Then the crisis in the oil patch hit with furious force for the following reasons:

1. Congressional approval of tax laws that removed incentives and disadvantaged the domestic industry in 1982 and 1986;
2. A glut of oil worldwide starting about 1982, primarily due to the tremendous expansion of exploration and production that followed price increases;
3. New and tougher environmental regulations on the domestic oil and gas industry.

And so, while the world price of oil fell dramatically, government-imposed production costs increased in the United States. Thousands of domestic producers were bankrupted or simply quit doing business. Imports skyrocketed once again—to 32 percent in 1986, 35 percent in 1988, 42 percent in 1989, and, by June 1992, 52 percent—over the halfway line for the first time in history.

But nobody outside the industry seemed to notice. Or they did not care. During the 1992 presidential campaigns, neither President George Bush nor then-candidate Bill Clinton discussed energy issues in a way that recognized the danger of our increased reliance on imported oil. We can only speculate as to the reasons, but suspect that President Bush did not want to acknowledge the problem because it had occurred on his watch as president; and candidate Clinton, for his part, was playing to the environmental, anti-oil audience. Both candidates made pronouncements about alternative fuels, about conservation, about the environment. But neither acknowledged the growing risks from over-reliance on foreign producers.

Instead of a rational discussion of energy policies, the American people, during the 1992 presidential campaigns, were treated to a rehash of many of the same old shibboleths about "reducing dependence" on foreign oil. The answers were always easy and pat: develop alternative sources, reduce demand through conservation measures and taxation of the domestic industry (a contradiction no one seemed to notice), increase the corporate average fuel efficiency (CAFE) minimums, and so on. The *Christian Science Monitor* reported in September 1992: "In this election year's broad discussion about the economy, one of the most pivotal issues has been virtually ignored: foreign-oil dependence and the need for a national energy policy. . . . Energy issues received a scant 13-line mention in the official Democratic platform. The GOP's counterpart, a 123-page document released at the Republican National Convention last month, devoted just three pages of generalities to the topic."[1] The 1992 presidential campaigns made it clear to the nation's independent oil and gas producers that their desperate situation would continue. In fact, it was about to get worse.

The Clinton administration has been pushing for new taxes that will make it even tougher for domestic oil and gas producers to survive, much less prosper. Even more hair-raising, the Clinton administration is developing an aid package to provide a healthy chunk of investment capital—some estimates range as high as $350 million—to develop the expansive Siberian oilfields of the former Soviet Union. And this is direct assistance; it does not include a planned loan of $2 billion from the U.S. Export-Import Bank that will allow Russia to buy much-needed oilfield equipment. This is not to criticize Clinton's decision to assist in the rehabilitation of the former Soviet Union. But it is to point out yet another careless national policy decision that works to the detriment of a vital domestic industry.

There is something almost breathtakingly brainless about spending U.S. tax dollars to develop Russian oil and gas fields while American independent domestic producers shut down operations in the United States, and while oilfield workers like Steve Allen, who helped free Kuwait's oil riches from Saddam Hussein's brutal grasp, are forced to live in near poverty because of national policies that penalize domestic producers.

The matter gets even worse when you examine one of the principal reasons the Clinton administration has given to justify spending money on the Siberian oilfields—to *increase* Russian petroleum exports to the United States in order to strengthen U.S. strategic petroleum reserves. Even more unbelievably, the Center for Strategic and International Studies has proposed that we finance repairs to the ailing Russian oil and gas industry with this same strategic reserve; that is, with money that has been set aside to stockpile oil in the event of a national emergency. The Russians would repay the financing by supplying oil for the U.S. strategic petroleum reserve once their wells had begun to produce again.

Have we reached such a point of economic weakness and political insanity that we are betting our strategic reserves on *any* foreign producer, much less a politically volatile Russia? Russian oil supplies could be interrupted at almost any time, not because of a Cold War hangover of hostility to the United States, but because of internal political instability made more dangerous by a dissatisfied military. Hostilities between the confederation sister states is not merely a remote possibility. To rely on future Russian oil supplies for our strategic petroleum reserve is a madness that defies understanding.

The proposed aid to Russia is also intensifying our own regional political friction. By encouraging more imports, whether intentionally or not, Washington is making energy-dependent states—those that favor cheap oil and stringent tax and environmental measures against the oil patch—even more vulnerable to the scheming of international petropolitics.

Already, according to a study by the independent Coalition for American Energy Security, the New England states rely on imported oil for 91 percent of their petroleum consumption. Delaware and Vermont use no domestic oil at all; 100 percent of their demand is supplied by foreign sources. Maine and New Hampshire each uses 96 percent imported oil.

And so it goes down the Atlantic Seaboard. In contrast, the seven-state area embracing Alaska, Arizona, California, Hawaii, Nevada, Washington, and Oregon imports only 7 percent of the oil used, down from 16 percent in 1980. But imports are expected to rise to 39 percent of total consumption by the year 2000 as Alaska's North Slope fields are depleted and new environmental restrictions on drilling hamper production in California. Even if these seven states do not currently import much oil, fully one-fifth of the fifty states now gets 80 percent or more of its oil from foreign producers. And the percentage is rising.

If supplies are interdicted in the future, as they have been in the past, for reasons totally unrelated to market supply and demand, the most harmful impact will fall on those regions that are most dependent on foreign oil. If this happens, and there is another world oil-shortage crisis, it can reasonably be predicted that not one of the parties responsible will accept or receive blame. These people—members of Congress from Northeastern states and their allies in the Bush and Clinton White House—will fault "the industry." And whatever the specious arguments, they will surely be parroted by too many in the media. The inevitable calls will then issue to fix the oil shortages—by increased government intervention and controls, which, of course, will make matters even worse.

In a rational market, whatever oil is imported should come from the nearest neighbor. If politically imposed limitations did not exist, the United States would buy all of its oil from Mexico[2] and South America, while European nations would buy their oil from the former Soviet Union and the Middle East.

But by adopting policies that encourage oil imports from the Pacific Rim, the Middle East, and the former Soviet Union, we have, in effect, signed a blank check to these producers. They can raise prices or cut off supplies for any political, religious, or military purposes they might wish to pursue. At the risk of some repetition, these foreign producers and their agendas must be scrutinized.

As noted earlier, the former Soviet Union, for one, cannot be trusted as a steady supplier. Nor, for that matter, can it be counted a major exporter of oil at the present time; in 1991, it exported only about 327,000 barrels of crude to the United States. That number might rise in the future, and almost certainly will if the Clinton administration's policies become reality, but at least two factors argue against putting too much reliance on Russia and its Siberian energy deposits.

The first, as pointed out, is the danger of civil unrest in the former Soviet Union, which will make it difficult for the Russians to maintain, much less increase, oil and gas production. This is partly because civil instability will impede investment in the U.S. technology and equipment the Russians need to develop their vast oil deposits. Few boards of directors would approve a major capital spending program in a region that stands a good chance of becoming nationalized or blown up by civil strife.

The second reason why it is imprudent to count on the former Soviet Union as a major oil supplier is that the price slide that struck a crushing blow to U.S. producers in the 1980s also did serious damage to the Russian economy, which was communist at the time. The decline in oil and gas export revenues required the Soviets to spend their precious, meager gold reserves on Western technology and food. These expenditures helped to keep the communist economy alive for a while, but they depleted national assets needed to keep a deteriorating oil and gas industry even marginally healthy. As a result, production is down more than 21 percent from 1988. Pumps break down with almost predictable regularity, and pipelines habitually spill a great deal of oil and gas. According to the *New York Times*, which quoted Russian news reports, Russian oil producers customarily lose one-third of the crude they pump because of pipeline leaks and "wasteful" refinery techniques.[3] Clearly, then, we cannot and should not depend on Russia to satisfy our domestic oil consumption and strategic reserve requirements.

Since our largest single foreign supplier is Saudi Arabia, another reprise is in order. In 1991, the Saudis shipped almost 623 million barrels of oil to the United States. That represented almost 30 percent of all U.S. oil imports, and slightly more than 10 percent of every gallon of crude oil we consumed that year for all purposes—autos, trucks, and airplanes, home heating, plastics manufacturing, industrial production, and so on.

Granted the Saudis are currently our friends—the Gulf War alliance kept the greedy Saddam from the Saudi oilfields—still, only twenty years ago, the Saudis (along with the Kuwaitis) were principal instigators of the embargo that severely restricted the flow of foreign oil to the United States because of our military aid to Israel. And the U.S.-Israeli alliance will continue to irritate Saudi Arabia. More important to the near future, however, is the matter of low oil prices.

The Saudis have no international trade assets other than energy and the banking wealth produced by its petroleum reserves. Nomadic camels and Arabian carpets are not international bestsellers. Even Saudi sand—the nation's most abundant natural resource—is too fine grained and smooth for manufacturing cement, glass, or other goods requiring product-specific silicate materials. Consequently, if Saudi Arabia's cash flow becomes too compressed, the first place it will look—the only place it can look—will be to its oil and gas.

Should the Saudis decide to raise prices, they would not act unilaterally, but get an agreement from other OPEC members to restrict exports, which would not only bump the world price of crude oil but impose an immense burden on the United States. In fact, the Saudis have been trying to accomplish just such a cooperative effort since the end of the Gulf War, our "friendship" notwithstanding. When, for example, the Clinton administration began studying new taxes on energy, the Saudis made it known that they would react with some hostility if those taxes included an import fee. An import fee, of course, could dilute OPEC's influence over the worldwide oil pricing systems. So far, the only barrier that has prevented the Saudis from persuading the OPEC cartel to reduce production and raise prices is that OPEC is too fragile and disjointed by self-interest and immediate cash needs to reach any sort of agreement.

Viewed historically, the OPEC cartel is a coalition that ebbs and flows according to its own interests, sometimes according to each nation, sometimes as a bloc. But OPEC will not die because its overriding interest is tied to coalition oil pricing. Even at the most intense moments of the war between Iraq and Iran, or during Desert Storm when Saudi Arabia was the key member of the allied joint venture, OPEC continued to operate more or less as usual. A real possibility exists that someday the OPEC nations will coordinate their production capabilities and strengths. If and when this occurs, the OPEC cartel will not only be able to control world oil prices, but control them to the extent of scaring off investment in oilfields where production is expensive. That is, the OPEC nations will be able to control not just the flow of oil to the United States but in the United States itself. They will be able to determine how much we can invest in our own energy industry.

But the more immediate question is: What would happen in the event of an OPEC restriction on selling oil to the United States? The answer is that just as in 1973, and again in 1979, energy prices would increase dramatically, sparking inflation, bringing higher unemployment, and heightening regional political rivalries.

We cannot count on a Saudi-dominated OPEC, or on the cartel's other largest oil-producing members—Iraq, Iran, and Libya, respectively, OPEC's second, fifth, and seventh largest members in terms of proven oil reserves. Any Western nation that voluntarily put its energy future in the hands of Teheran's ayatollahs, Saddam Hussein, and Moammar Khadaffi would richly deserve its fate.

Nor could more stable nations make up a shortfall—at least not quickly. Energy drives the world, not just the United States, and most of the non-OPEC nations with large reservoirs of oil produce largely for their own consumption, and already export substantially to the United States.

Canada, for example, provided us with about 271.4 million barrels in 1991. Yet Canada still produces less than it consumes. We cannot count on Canada.

Mexico is another large non-OPEC supplier of crude to the United States. In 1991, Mexico sold us 277 million barrels of oil. This spigot could be opened to provide more oil and gas in the event of an OPEC withdrawal, but not enough to make up a severe shortfall. And this assumes that Mexico would provide us with energy at reasonable

prices—rather than demand nonenergy political and economic concessions.

And, in any event, why should Mexico or any other nation sell us oil
at less than the prevailing world price? Certainly the United States
would not do so if the tables were reversed.

Great Britain . . . Norway . . . Angola . . . all exported between 50
and 100 million barrels of oil each year to the United States in 1991.
Again, these countries probably could increase exports, but not
enough to keep prices down in the event an oil shortage prompted by
an embargo on OPEC exports.

Another aspect of our dependence is that it undercuts our power to
bargain for free trade agreements with nations that supply us with oil
yet have erected trade barriers against U.S. goods.

For example, in late March 1993 the Clinton administration accused
forty-four nations of unfair trade practices, practices that work against
U.S. export interests. Among the nations were Colombia, which exported 44.9 million barrels of oil to the United States in 1991; Ecuador,
which sold us 19.2 million barrels; Venezuela, 244 million barrels;
Nigeria, 249 million barrels; Indonesia, 37.2 million barrels; and Norway, 27 million barrels. Altogether, twelve of the nations on the State
Department list provided us with 907.5 million barrels of oil in 1991, or
almost 43 percent of all of the oil we imported. It will be difficult to deal
with these nations as long as they have the upper hand.

The inescapable fact is that we have become so dependent on foreign
oilfields that we are today in danger of becoming seriously weakened as
an international political superpower. The evidence that oil currently
drives international politics is overwhelming. As Daniel Yergin noted in
THE PRIZE, you can make a good argument that both of this century's major wars were fought for oil. In World War I, it was over oil to
fuel the mammoth dreadnoughts built by Great Britain and Imperial
Germany in a naval arms race as costly to civilian economics as the Cold
War was forty years later. In World War II, it was Japan's grasp for the
rich oilfields of Southeast Asia, and Adolf Hitler's desire to control the
Rumanian fields at Ploesti and the enormous Soviet energy deposits in

the Saratov, Volgorod, and Kalmuck fields north of Georgian Baku on the Caspian Sea.[4]

It would be naive to think that today's aspirants for political domination or influence are any different from Imperial Germany at the turn of the century or Nazi Germany and an expansionist Japan in the 1930s and 1940s. A recent example is Saddam Hussein's savage mugging of Kuwait to gain ascendancy over the Middle Eastern oilfields. Consequently, the United States should be doing everything possible to control its own energy destiny rather than bowing to the political influence of OPEC and other Third World nations.

Nor is this the only cause for concern.

Another is the increasing ownership of U.S. refining capacity by foreign investors. The U.S. refining industry is being all but forced to sit by and watch the deterioration of plant and equipment that has made it necessary to seek foreign investors to upgrade them. This development is also linked to a decline in the U.S. oil patch. It is another example of how federal tax and environmental policies have made it unprofitable for domestic investors to own domestic oil and gas properties.

A principal reason for this, once again, is tougher environmental regulations that require new equipment. It will take an estimated $20 billion, minimum, to upgrade U.S. refineries to meet the standards demanded by the amendments to the Clean Air Act of 1990. This means huge new sums of investment capital must be raised, and U.S. oil and gas companies are justifiably leery about government promises allowing them to earn a return sufficient to warrant putting money into the U.S. refining industry. Experience has taught domestic investors that such promises are too often illusory.

As a result, foreign capital is filling the void in the U.S. refining industry. According to oil analyst Bernard Picchi of the Kidder, Peabody investment banking firm in New York City, almost 10 percent of the nation's 15.5 million barrels per day refining capacity is now owned by foreign investors.[5] Picchi claims that the likely investors (in addition to Mexico and Venezuela) include Saudi Arabia and Norway.

By making ourselves dependent upon foreign producers for our ravenous thirst for oil, we are handing a club to multitudes of foreign policymakers who will surely wield it in support of their political purposes.

The nightmare is not something for future generations to fear. The cruel reality may be a tomorrow for us. And then every American will feel the pain.

Meanwhile, Steve Allen has abandoned hope of finding work in the oil patch in the United States. Instead, he's sending out resumes to dozens of companies, majors and independents alike, applying for work in foreign fields. If he is accepted, he says he will move his family from Oklahoma to almost any overseas location—just to work in the oil industry. And the U.S. oil patch will be that much poorer for having lost one more skilled worker who answered when his nation called, returning only to find that his nation had forced his company to export his job. It is a sad commentary on the national policies that control the oil and gas industry and on what it has done to the people who serve its vital purposes.

CHAPTER EIGHT

THE WAGES OF IMPRUDENCE
PART III

THE SOCIAL COST OF KILLING
A BASIC INDUSTRY

In superficial ways, Patrick F. Taylor of New Orleans fits some people's stereotyped image of an oilman.

First there is the exterior impression, which is misleading. Pat Taylor dresses the part of a Southwestern oilman, rancher, and ex-rodeo performer. His impeccably stylish attire includes highly polished cowboy boots and designer suspenders, his wardrobe signature. His suits and ties have a clear, sharp, Western look. Behind the clothing stands a tall, graying, handsome man in his middle fifties with a military posture. The only accessory missing from the stereotypical picture is a large cigar; smoking is eschewed by Pat Taylor following heart difficulties several years ago. From outward impressions alone, Pat Taylor, with his good looks and confident bearing, would appear to be perfect for the part of an independent oil producer in any Hollywood movie.

In real life Pat Taylor likes being rich, as would most of us. He relishes money and it shows—airplanes, helicopters, a chauffeured limousine. He was an ardent parachutist, a hobby he took up in his early thirties and continued until he had made almost six hundred jumps—about five hundred more than most parachutists.

But Taylor didn't grow up with wealth. He was raised in modest, almost poor circumstances in Beaumont and Houston, Texas. He spent his summers during his high school years as a roustabout in the East Texas oilfields, where he developed a lifelong affection for the oil and gas industry. "All I've ever wanted to be is an oilman," he says.

Taylor's relationship with his stepfather, a watchmaker, was stormy. At sixteen, even before graduating from high school, he was summarily kicked out of his home, a wrenching emotional experience. But he managed to arrange his own scholarship at an exclusive private academy in Houston and graduated with honors.

Determined to go to college but unable to pay tuition, Taylor went to New Orleans in 1956 at age eighteen. He had been told two important facts about Louisiana State University—the school had an excellent petroleum engineering school, and, just as important, LSU did not charge tuition. What he did not know was that the tuition-free privilege extended only to Louisiana residents. When he reached New Orleans, Taylor had only $55 in his pocket. Even so, because of his excellent high school record, he was able to talk his way into a tuition-free education. At LSU, he completed work on his degree in petroleum geology in only three years.

Since then, he has accumulated millions of dollars—not the $185 million estimated by Forbes magazine in 1991, but substantial wealth—by pumping oil and gas from the rich energy deposits off Louisiana's Gulf Coast. Today, Taylor Energy Co. of New Orleans, with some thirty offshore platform rigs, is one of the largest independent oil and gas producers operating in the Gulf of Mexico.

If anyone has earned the title of "independent" in the business, it's Pat Taylor. He has created his business with no outside investors, no stockholders, no limited investment partners. When he borrows money, only his name is listed on the loan agreement. He has taken all of the financial risks of his oil and gas exploration and production efforts, and, fittingly, has enjoyed most of the rewards.

But something sets Pat Taylor apart from the stereotype of an oil-patch energy baron—some people would call it a "social conscience." However named, it has prompted Pat Taylor to give of his wealth in order to provide college educations for economically disadvantaged kids, most of them minorities, who otherwise would have little hope of escaping the brutal cycle of inner-city poverty, crime, and ignorance.

Put starkly, Pat Taylor, a wealthy, white, conservative, Republican, independent oil and gas producer, is spending his personal wealth to put poor black, Hispanic, and other minority students through college. It is hardly the picture of a greedy, self-serving oilman. Pat Taylor himself rejects the notion that his philanthropy stems from a "social conscience." His reason for doing what he does, he says, is the simple recognition that without a tuition-free education at LSU, his life would have been very, very different. And for this he is grateful.

His assistance to poor students began in 1988 when he was giving a speech to about 180 seventh- and eighth-graders at a New Orleans middle school located in a neighborhood awash in a sea of drugs and ravaged by crime. Many of these kids had already failed one or two grades and were simply waiting to drop out of school. Taylor was struck with the plight of the students, most of whom appeared to be bright enough to acquire an education—to break a lifestyle of poverty and deprivation—but seemed to have little incentive to do so.

So he made the kids a deal: if they graduated with a B average, he would see that they attended one of Louisiana's state universities. He then enlisted additional financial backing for the plan among leaders of the New Orleans business community. Three years later, twenty-six of the eighth graders, now calling themselves "Taylor's Kids," were high school seniors, preparing to get a higher education.

That was just the beginning. Since then, having seen the tremendous impact a promise of college had on "Taylor's Kids," he has actively promoted the "Taylor Plan," a state law that provides tuition at state universities for poverty-level high school students with satisfactory testing achievement scores and a 2.5 grade-point average in a high school curric-ulum aimed at a career in business, science, or the professions. Louisiana's legislature was the first to adopt the plan in 1989. Since then Taylor has appeared before state legislatures across the nation to argue for the "Taylor Plan," or some variation of it. And he has been successful; by 1993, twelve other states had approved similar legislation.[1]

In short, Pat Taylor has freely invested his considerable personal and management skills, along with the wealth earned from his oil and gas *business, to provide an education for economically disadvantaged but academically qualified and well-motivated young people. As a result, he has not only given hope to these students, but has also helped society, which will improve as these students enter the workforce and become contributing members of it.*

It could be argued, of course, that if Pat Taylor had not made his money in the oil and gas business he would have done so elsewhere. Entrepreneurial creativity is usually an adaptable, transferable skill. And, given his obvious commitment to helping other people, whatever the line of work he might have chosen Pat Taylor probably would have assisted others in some fashion or another.

But Pat Taylor *did* make his fortune as an independent oil and gas producer. He *did* share that wealth with disadvantaged young people. And, as a result, society *has* benefitted from the riches provided by the earth's hydrocarbon deposits and the social conscience of one oilman. Moreover, Pat Taylor did all of this voluntarily, not through forced taxation. This leads to the next point:

Economics propels much of human activity and provides a basic foundation for social improvement and political stability. Economic wealth is essential to social betterment, just as economic poverty is a root factor in causing social and environmental deterioration.

Political systems, for their part, are profoundly influenced by economics, perhaps more so today than ever before, due to instant worldwide communications and the global nature of economics. A government or political system must provide an economic base to sustain itself. Granted, economic prosperity can be accompanied by moral decay. But this is a separate issue. The fact is, human history has no record of economic wealth alone destroying a civilization. But it teems with examples of political systems and governments that have fallen because of economic distress.

Recent history proves this point: the collapse of communism in the former Soviet Union and its satellite nations was due to the failure of communism's economic and political philosophy. Even more recently, and a less extreme example: former President George Bush was defeated in 1992 largely on a single issue—economics. The sign that hung in Governor Clinton's Arkansas campaign headquarters during the 1992 race said it all: "IT'S THE ECONOMY, STUPID."

All of which leads to the important reason why today's crisis in America's oil patch is a national, even an international, social, political, and economic problem and not just a regional economic decline affecting only the oil-producing areas of the United States.

If we allow the U.S. oil and gas industry to continue its headlong plunge toward disaster, the social consequences could affect every level of society and all parts of the world. It has already begun in the energy-dependent communities in the United States, where economic depression has been followed by social deterioration. Given our growing dependence on foreign oil, what would happen if the energy tap suddenly was slowed or turned off? Similar deterioration of social services would hit nationwide. This would be accompanied by higher tax burdens to make up for the loss of tax contributions from the U.S. energy industry and other industries that depend upon it to survive. Which is to say most industries. Higher taxes in a failing economy would worsen the problem—an essential truth that some politicians seem incapable of understanding.

Ultimately, the impact would be felt globally as U.S. producers for overseas markets found themselves priced out of business. In turn, foreign suppliers of U.S. markets would lose their once-prosperous customers. International politics could become even more chaotic if an economically weakened United States could not sustain a diplomatic and military presence befitting the world's only remaining superpower.

Imagine a small community of 100,000 people or so. Place it anywhere in America's heartland—Kansas, or Vermont, Georgia, even Puerto Rico or Guam. All of these, along with the other states, U.S. possessions, and the District of Columbia, constitute America's heartland.

This community—call it Anywhere, U.S.A.—is prosperous, but not overly so. It has a shopping mall and an industrial park, whose major tenant produces light industrial machinery for the paper and packaging industry. This plant employs, say, two thousand people, the community's largest single employer. The plant injects a payroll of perhaps $50 million annually into the local economy.

From that relatively narrow base the economic benefit flows outward. It spreads to sustain barbershops, real estate offices, video-rental shops, supermarkets, convenience stores, new- and used-auto dealerships, construction industries, several banks, and a few law firms, to name just some of a modern community's economic factors.

From here, the economic benefits expand: $50 million in payroll at the manufacturing plant directly generates perhaps as much as $250 million in other employment contributions to the economic system. That sum enlarges as the wealth is shared, creating an overall economic base of $1 billion or more—in a community of just 100,000 people. And this is just payroll. It does not include the additional $2–3 billion more in property evaluations that provide a basis for tax revenues from a modestly prosperous population.

Tax revenues on this income and property in Anywhere, U.S.A., support social services that include education for young people, police and fire protection, garbage collection, sewage disposal, community recreation facilities, parks, and a library system. In short, a society's basic needs and optional comforts are wholly dependent upon local economic prosperity.

Anywhere, U.S.A., would be a congenial place to live in if it existed in a vacuum. But today there are no economic, social, and political islands. The prosperity of the plant that provides the economic basis for the entire community depends on factors far beyond the control of its management.

To be sure, management can set goals for sales and profit growth. It can negotiate local labor contracts, establish expense controls, develop marketing plans, and take other steps to meet those objectives. If it could be left solely to local management, the plant would probably continue to operate profitably, feeding the economy of the community.

But the community's economy and social structure cannot be decided locally. Any number of external factors determine the economic prosperity of Anywhere, U.S.A., and all of them have a sharp impact on the community. Decisions made in Riyadh, Saudi Arabia, in Tehran, Iran, in Caracas, Venezuela, in Mexico City, Mexico, can influence the quality of life in Anywhere, U.S.A., because they can dramatically affect the cost and availability of energy. Energy is the most basic determinant of Anywhere, U.S.A.'s, local economy, and, hence, of its social structure.

The first warnings for Anywhere, U.S.A., came when the Arab nations agreed to limit production and boost the price of crude petroleum exports by 30 percent. Energy prices began spiraling upward. Every nation on the globe was affected, but none as critically as the United States, the world's largest industrial economy and, therefore, the world's largest consumer of energy. Imports dropped sharply as prices rose and the nation tried to reduce demand. But changing people's basic lifestyles—such as their energy consumption—cannot be accomplished in a week or a month or even a year.

And so the nation's consumers paid the escalating prices as unleaded gasoline soared above $2 a gallon with no end in sight. Foreign producers, seeing how easily a tiger's tail could be twisted, began to turn the spigot even tighter, which boosted prices even more.

But the horror story was just beginning. With the domestic energy industry crippled by taxation and excessive regulation, U.S. oil producers had lost all interest in seeking new hydrocarbon sources to offset the need for foreign oil. And even if independent U.S. producers had been able economically to look for new sources of energy, they would by this point have lacked sufficient trained personnel and operable exploratory and production equipment to do so. During the past years, employment in the oil patch had dropped to the bare minimum required to keep existing wells pumping; hundreds of thousands of geologists, roustabouts, and tool-pushers had found work in new industries. The exploration and production rigs that once sprouted so profusely in the oil patch were rusting in junkyards, or had been dismantled to keep existing machinery operating. New domestic oil and gas reserves could not quickly or easily be developed to replace American reliance on foreign oil.

Then, under pressure from militant fundamentalist members of OPEC, Middle Easterners, squeezing the flow even more, insisted that the U.S. government moderate its political and military support of Israel if it wanted to continue receiving Arabian Gulf oil. This put more upward pressure on prices. Other Third World OPEC nations, realizing the vulnerability of the United States, joined the Middle Eastern nations by demanding trade concessions and other benefits in return for crude oil from the Pacific Rim, South America, and other large producing areas. Meantime, higher energy prices accelerated the rate of decline of U.S. domestic industrial production and exports, ballooning the trade deficit even more.

Here is how this imaginary scenario affects people—imaginary or real. In our imaginary community of Anywhere, U.S.A.—as in the real world of 1973 and 1979—long lines of vehicles began to form around gasoline pumps as drivers waited impatiently for their share of the reduced supplies of the expensive gasoline. That was just the beginning of the distress—and relatively minor. Like all other basic manufacturing industries, the paper and packaging business began to feel the pinch of higher fuel prices and had to cut back on orders for new processing machinery. This had a direct, immediate, and hard impact on Anywhere, U.S.A., far more serious than waiting in line for unleaded gasoline. It meant a reduction in the community's workforce.

At first, the employment reduction was small, maybe no more than 10 percent, about two hundred workers. But as fuel supplies got tighter, the plant's own energy costs began to soar. This pushed operating expenses higher at a time when demand for the plant's products was falling. Employment layoffs grew from a trickle to a torrent, as the plant's worried managers began to plan for the bleak months ahead until the energy shortage abated . . . maybe.

Then the entire community began to feel the pinch. As employment declined at the fabricating plant, the economic ripples became a whirlpool that threatened the community's entire socioeconomic fabric. Unemployment costs skyrocketed as jobless workers jammed the office where unemployment applications and checks were processed. Homeowners who had lost their jobs began to put their property on the market, but there were no buyers. Some property owners simply mailed their keys to the mortgage lender and walked away, moving to other parts of the country in a futile search for work. Commercial real estate values plummeted along with residential properties. Strip-shopping centers began to empty. Banks and other mortgage lenders wrote off millions of dollars in lost real estate loans. Lending institutions approached Washington for financial rescue.

Property tax collections fell dramatically. The local school system began consolidating, cutting back programs. Police and fire departments became overworked and undermanned as tax receipts dried up, and this at a time when the crime rate was rising alarmingly—a social phenomenon that accompanies unemployment.

And so it went.

In short, after the initial OPEC pricing action and subsequent interruption of supplies, Anywhere, U.S.A., was well down the road toward a severe economic depression that had far-reaching social consequences. The community would never be the same. Lives had been disrupted, educations abandoned, social services reduced; the community's infrastructure had deteriorated and its population now lived in straitened economic conditions. And it all stemmed from U.S. vulnerability to foreign oil producers who controlled the nation's price of energy.

This imaginary example is oversimplified, of course, but it is not unrealistic. On the contrary, *it has already happened.* The disaster has struck many oil-patch communities, which have been victimized by national policies that have encouraged oil imports rather than the development of the domestic oil and gas industry. The following economic indicators show a serious social decline in the nation's major oil-producing states, beginning with the oil crisis that began about 1982 and expanded throughout the decade.[2]

- In Alaska, revenues from state severance taxes declined by about $300 million between 1985 and 1990, to $1.1 billion from $1.4 billion. This money is used to supply social services, educate children, provide health care, and construct roads, bridges, and highways.
- On a percentage basis, the decline in Louisiana was even more severe, with severance tax collections dropping more than 40 percent, to $429.1 million in 1990 from $745.2 million five years earlier. Texas and Oklahoma were just as bad, losing an annual $1.1 billion and $313.5 million, respectively, or almost half their total tax revenues from oil and gas production. This does not include

lost property tax revenues for both local and state governments, which depleted public treasuries by billions of dollars while the cost of social services was rising.

- As unemployment soared in the oil-patch states in the 1980s, the public cost of caring for jobless workers and their families increased accordingly. In Texas, for example, between 1985 and 1990, the number of people receiving federal food stamps grew by 743,000, an increase of 62 percent in just five years.

- Between 1980 and 1990, disposable personal income *fell* by about 1 percent in Oklahoma at the same time as it was *rising* by almost 17 percent nationwide.

- In Colorado, the median family income dropped 10 percent between 1985 and 1990. In Louisiana, the decline was almost 13 percent. Similar, although not so severe, decreases in median family income were also recorded in Oklahoma, Texas, and Alaska. During the same period, a time that saw the onset of a national recession, median family income nationwide rose by more than 4 percent.

- The percentage of people living in poverty nationwide, according to the U.S. Bureau of the Census, declined by half a percentage point nationwide, to 13.5 percent in 1990 from 14.0 percent five years earlier. In the oil patch, however, the number of poor people grew dramatically—in Oklahoma, to 15.6 percent from 13.3 percent; in Louisiana, to 23.6 percent from 18.1 percent; in Colorado, to 13.2 percent from 10.2 percent. Texas, with its broader economic base, was luckier; the percentage of people living below the poverty level there remained flat at 15.9 percent.

Poverty is not a problem just for poor people, because poverty requires public expenditures to care for the jobless and their families. This money is withdrawn from a system of social spending that could help educate children, reduce prison populations, and so on.

Take Texas in the decade between 1980 and 1990.

To begin with, in the Texas oil patch, more was admittedly at work than just a decline in the domestic energy industry. In Texas, the rolling recession of the 1990s began about 1982, slowly gathering momentum until it peaked there around 1988. This recession was created by numerous factors, such as the federal banking policies that spurred the $500 billion collapse of the nation's savings and loan industry.

But the nation's energy policies probably began the downward roll in Texas. In the early 1980s Texas banks were heavily involved in energy lending. When oil and gas prices began falling due to oversupply of cheap oil by foreign producers, and when new U.S. tax laws reduced incentives for investment in domestic exploration and production, Southwestern U.S. banks began calling in energy loans and replacing them with real estate loans. Real estate developers, encouraged by the rising energy prices during the 1979–82 period, had in the meantime been pouring concrete and building huge office towers as if there were no tomorrow.

The problem, of course, was that all of this activity depended on an ongoing, prosperous energy industry. Energy was what sustained the Southwestern U.S. real estate industry. But the harsh realities of 1986 and a bottoming of oil prices—not to mention stern tax laws that inhibited investment in both real estate and energy—shattered that foundation. This too could have been nothing more than a regional problem, except for one factor: banks nationwide had bought the illusion that even if energy were dead (a real illusion: the United States has plenty of recoverable oil and gas) real estate was alive and growing. From California to Washington State to New England to the South, bankers scurried to buy participations in Southwestern real estate loans that had replaced energy lending.

And so the energy industry, then real estate, then banking, then scores of other businesses, not just in Texas but nationwide, began sliding into insolvency. It was the beginning of a trend that soon struck with cruel force in the Northeast, the Southeast, the Midwest, and finally the West Coast.

And it all began with energy. The energy industry is critical to Texas, Louisiana, and Oklahoma, but these states do not stand alone. On the contrary, as we have tried to point out in these pages, U.S. energy reserves are vital to the entire national economy—to the world economy. To understand how our social fabric can be ripped by what boils down to dependence on foreign oil, consider these changes in the social structure of Texas in the 1980s. Some of them were reported by the *Dallas Morning News* in a thoughtful report in April 1993:[3]

- Violent crimes committed by juveniles in Texas increased by 45 percent between 1982 and 1991, to 105,665 felonies in 1991 from 72,705 nine years earlier.
- According to economic data from the Census Bureau, the number of people in Texas living below the poverty level grew by more than 500,000 in the decade of the 1980s, to 2.7 million in 1990 from 2.2 million ten years earlier. This represented fully half the increase of 1 million people who slipped below the poverty line nationwide during the decade. (Another point: While the actual number of people living in poverty nationwide increased between 1980 and 1990, the percentage of the population making less than a living wage declined. This was in contrast to Texas, where the ratio grew.)
- During that same time, demands for social services increased. To make up for the lack of money needed to meet local needs, between 1981–82 and 1991–92, local property tax receipts more than doubled, although the property tax base grew only 18 percent.
- Educational test scores in public schools fell. Prisons became crowded, law forces were strained, and basic social services were overworked.

As stated earlier, not all of this resulted from the decline in the oil patch. But national policies did nothing to prevent or offset the adverse impact of the predatory pricing of foreign oil—the beginning of the downturn. Just as oil and gas were basic to creating prosperity in Texas, so their decline marked the beginning of the state's regression in economic affluence and social well-being.

Moreover, this same decline—the decline in domestic oil and gas exploration—might well have been a root cause of the nation's deteriorating social services and lifestyles. *Put simply, dependence on foreign oil can trigger a national economic and social degeneration—even though the United States has abundant energy riches.*

This is not a lament for the adversities that have beset Texas, Oklahoma, Louisiana, and the other oil-patch states. The tears have already been shed. Steve Allen, who fought in the Gulf War to protect

Kuwait's oilfields only to find that he had no job in the oil patch when he came home, has learned to live on less than half the money he earned as a roustabout in Oklahoma. Sonny Lowery gets along on the few dollars he earns sweeping parking lots free of beer cans and broken bottles. Pat Nelson, the petroleum geologist, is making an adequate living selling eye-glass frames. Independent oil and gas producer Robert Gunn, Pat Nelson's former boss, has moved much of his capital overseas where oil and gas can be pumped more cheaply than in his own backyard.

The intention is not to deplore a crisis that has already hit but to stop it from spreading nationwide, even globally—to change U.S. policies. Depending upon foreign producers for any more of our future energy supplies than is absolutely necessary—indeed, increasing that reliance—is an enormous mistake.

The United States is the only remaining economic and military superpower. Without our leadership, the world's political stability is at risk. We have seen it happen in Eastern Europe, following the collapse of the Soviet Union. Today, a prosperous United States can help drive the commercial, manufacturing, and financial engines of the more industrial as well as developing nations.

But all of this economic and social power rests on energy. Energy is behind the nation's agricultural machinery that feeds starving people in Somalia, the former Soviet Union, Southeast Asia, and Central Europe. If people cannot eat, they cannot survive to create their own prosperity. The social fabric of entire nations depends on the threads sewn by the United States, and those threads were woven on the loom of energy.

Petroleum products fuel transportation in the United States. Transportation, in turn, serves as both a market for and carrier of products of the great industries that benefit U.S. business and provide a higher standard of living for consumers in Western Europe, Japan, the Pacific Rim, Central and South America, the Middle East, and elsewhere. Without those consumer goods and other products churned out by U.S. industries, and without the enormous U.S. market, our allies among the more industrialized nations would find their own standards of living falling, their job opportunities restricted, and their social structures degenerating. Without the economic power of the United States, many more people could starve in Africa, Russia could revert to grinding poverty, and Middle Eastern nations could see the escalation of traditional hostilities between Moslems and Jews—to name but a few looming crises.

As a nation, the United States is making its economy dependent on the goodwill of political and economic leaders in the Middle East, South America, and the Pacific Rim. It is not just a hazardous, dangerous course. It is near suicidal.

It is no overstatement to say that we are committing the national equivalent of *hara-kiri* by continuing to allow our own abundant oil and gas reserves to lie fallow, victims of repressive tax and environmental regulations, while we rely on the hydrocarbon deposits of foreign governments.

DONALD PAUL HODEL:
One of the hardest problems I faced in writing this book was dealing with the role that I and the Reagan administration and its policies had had in contributing to the downfall of this great industry. There was, perhaps, no industry more supportive of President Reagan. As Secretary of Energy and as Secretary of the Interior, I benefitted from that support on numerous trips to the oil patch. Key producers, independents and majors alike, could not have been more cordial or encouraging. They cautioned, however, about what was happening in the oil and gas industry as the rig count began to fall. Then, as the situation worsened, at about the time I left the Department of Energy in early 1985, the warnings became much more urgent. Yet, it was unthinkable within the administration to take any actions that could have been characterized as "protectionist."

We did attempt to assist in ideologically acceptable ways. As Secretary of the Interior, I was responsible for the oil and gas leases on federal land and provided as much relief as possible within the rules of law. During that time, the price of oil fell so low that leases would have been forfeited if the rules had been applied stringently. In Cabinet Council discussions, I also favored the retention of tax incentives for oil and gas drilling, as well as the retention of tax incentives for renewables and conservation. (All these tax incentives were removed by the 1986 act.)

Much of my effort as Secretary of the Interior involved trying to make available for exploration and development promising areas of the western United States, Alaska, and the outer continental shelf. But the tide was running against us, and we had little to show for all the anguish and effort my staff and I expended.

Finally, early in 1985 as the price of oil was plunging, I personally prepared charts and graphs supporting the idea of an "Import Security Premium" of $3 to $5 per barrel on imported oil. After all, I reasoned, our administration supported users' fees on all kinds of activities—including access to our national parks. Why should the purchaser of gasoline get a free insurance policy called the Strategic Petroleum Reserve? It meant that he could buy gasoline for 10 cents or 15 cents a gallon less than the "real" cost for SPR—plus the cost of our military presence in the Middle East.

I took the charts with me to a cabinet breakfast. These periodically held breakfasts were presided over by the chief of staff and attended by cabinet officers only. They were the most open and free of all cabinet sessions; unlike other cabinet meetings, the subjects discussed were not leaked to the press. That day twelve members were in attendance. I made my pitch. The only spoken response came from Secretary of State George Schultz, who opined that my idea might be viewed as contrary to GATT. No one else even commented.

When I returned to my office, I told my staff that if it had been put to a vote, the measure would have failed—none in favor, eleven against, and one abstaining. I could see where the wind was blowing.

The result of all these efforts was zilch. The industry continued to face increasingly tough times.

The cries of anguish from the oil and gas industry were muted by a number of factors. Fundamentally, the men and women in the oil and gas industry were strongly independent and did not want government assistance; they were, by and large, great fans of President Reagan and did not want to do or say anything that might be interpreted as critical of him; very few people in or out of the industry understood the magnitude of the threat to the industry; and, finally, the disastrous price slide that reached its bottom in the spring of 1986 could not have been reasonably anticipated.

Having said all that, I find myself thinking back over the process to see where we might have acted effectively to avoid or dilute the catastrophe that has fallen on America's oil and gas industry. As members of the administration, we were committed, as were many in the industry itself, to avoiding arbitrary governmental interference in a "free" market.

Although we knew it to be true, I believe we inadequately took into account the fact that, thanks to OPEC, the world oil market is not a free market. Furthermore, in retrospect, it seems that we should have foreseen that a world oil price collapse would devastate the U.S. industry, and that such a price collapse could not be caused by a truly free market because a very large segment of that market is controlled by OPEC. If we had taken that view, we might have been able to prevent the harmful impacts of predatory pricing. In fact, I did try to prevent this but was unable to obtain administration support.

But another factor also came into play. At the time that our "free market" language befogged our view of the world oil picture, we were under constant attack from the environmental Left for not displacing oil usage with environmentally benign—or, in today's terminology, "politically correct"—energy sources. The environmentalist domination of the media, the Democratic majority in the House of Representatives, and key members of the Democratic minority in the Senate (until 1986, when matters became even worse as the Democrats regained control of the Senate) made it difficult, if not impossible, to pursue pro-oil patch policies.

I conclude reluctantly that even if we had been able to foresee accurately the consequences to millions of Americans of doing nothing to avert the impending crisis, we could not at that time have created a strategy that would have had a chance of success in the anti-oil, progreen political atmosphere that prevailed.

To this pervasive hostility I attribute the fact that nearly 500,000 direct jobs can be lost in the oil patch with nary a squawk in Washington, while a few thousand jobs lost in the auto, steel, or textile industries generate howls of distress. The mere threat of Chrysler's failure produced government loan guarantees worth billions of dollars. What would comparable support have meant for the domestic oil and gas industry?

Solutions exist. We can reduce our dependence on foreign oil and encourage our domestic economy and thereby maintain and strengthen the national social infrastructure that supports public education, police and fire protection, and other vital public services. And all of this can be done without endangering the environment.

Ironically, the environment itself has been hard hit by the decline of the U.S. oil and gas industry. Oil and gas exploration and production can have an adverse environmental impact in some areas, but overall the energy industry contributes billions of dollars annually to maintaining and improving the environment. You hear much from industry opponents about environmental crimes committed by the oil and gas industry but little about what the industry spends each year to improve it.

The total amount spent by the industry in 1992 on environmental concerns was $8 billion. To put this number in perspective, it was almost as much as the industry spent on domestic exploration for oil and gas, and almost a third more than the entire federal budgetary allocation of approximately $5.9 billion for the Environmental Protection Agency. The $8 billion was, in fact, about 30 percent more than the total $6.1 billion spent by all federal government agencies in 1992 on pollution control and abatement.

Critics might argue that these dollars were spent only to sanitize earlier contamination by oil and gas producers. Not so. Billions of dollars *were* spent on cleaning up old drilling sites and meeting stringent local, state, and federal environmental standards on the existing sites. But, at the same time, significant sums were spent on research and development of cleaner fuels ($175 million). Meantime, the private sector made efforts to remove high-pollution vehicles from our roadways, planted trees, and made other environmental improvements ($147 million), all voluntarily.

Clearly, the oil and gas industry provides the nation with more than just the energy it requires to maintain a vibrant economy and strong social structure. In addition, it makes important contributions to our social fabric—among them, maintaining a clean environment.

The means to rescue the oil patch are not complicated. But neither are they easy. Revitalizing America's energy industry will require strong political leadership and a vigorous national will to carry it out. It is not too late to act. But the clock is ticking down. And if present trends are not reversed, the consequences will be felt at all levels of society.

CHAPTER NINE

CRISIS IN THE OIL PATCH

WHAT MUST BE DONE TO SAVE A VITAL INDUSTRY

Over the previous pages we have tried to show the harmful impact of the many burdens imposed on the oil patch. We have sought to demonstrate how these have strangled a vital industry and severely damaged the lives of hundreds of thousands of people. Every one of these burdens has been a disincentive to investing in the search for oil and gas in the United States.

Yet if people do not look for oil and gas, none will be found. And the search must go on if we want to create jobs, produce domestic wealth, and reduce import dependence—that is, maintain our economic strength which, in turn, sustains our global political leadership.

Alternative fuels can and should continue to be developed, of course, especially where they reduce our dependence on hydrocarbon energy. Every type of alternative energy that replaces hydrocarbons,[1] like every barrel of oil produced in the United States, reduces our import dependence.

But alternatives have had little success, even with the federal subsidies and special incentives given the alternative-fuel producers. In part, this is because of the relatively low cost of the oil they must replace. More importantly, perhaps, is the fear investors have that foreign suppliers—especially OPEC—will "yo-yo" the price of oil down low enough and long enough to dissipate the value of investments in the domestic U.S. oil and gas industry. Sustained low oil prices would of course harm alternative-fuels development. At $10 a barrel, for example, foreign oil would be cheaper than any domestic alternative.

Moreover, at present technological levels, all of the combined alternative fuels would not yield enough energy for our needs.

Methanol, for example, has lower energy-per-unit than gas or oil. Ethanol is worse: it yields less energy than it takes to produce it. And that most ideal of fuels—hydrogen—takes a prohibitive amount of energy to produce (at the present state of technology). Electricity, of course, is not an "alternative" fuel. It is an energy form produced by other energy sources.

While it is important and desirable—even necessary—for the United States to seek to reduce oil dependence by every reasonable means, including alternative fuels, certainly for the next two decades or so, oil and gas will continue to supply most of America's energy needs.

Yet, burdensome federal tax and regulatory policies continue to scare off investors from financing exploration for new domestic deposits of oil and gas. In fact, the big companies believe, with some justification, that they have been the victims of an "expulsion of capital," that because of tax and environmental policies, they have been forced to go overseas to look for new sources of oil and gas. Major companies have increased their investment—and their employment base—overseas.

The major energy companies that do continue to invest in domestic drilling do so under limited conditions: developmental drilling must be done in proven fields, that is, where oil and gas are known to exist; and drilling begins only when the chances of finding huge new pools of oil are better than average. Thus the public is misled about the extent of America's rich energy deposits by the occasional headline announcing a significant new discovery, because most of these are not strictly "new." They are located in such proven oil-rich regions as Alaska's North Slope.

All available data show that the major oil companies have all but stopped looking for new oil and gas in the original forty-eight states.

According to the American Petroleum Institute, in 1992 U.S. producers invested 65% of their exploration and production dollars overseas, and only 35% in the United States. This was a 180-degree turnaround from 1982, when the ratio was 33% overseas and 67% domestically.

Instead of spending capital to create jobs and pump oil at home, they are selling existing domestic fields to raise money, a significant portion of which goes into overseas ventures. The buyers of these producing fields are the smaller independents such as Taylor Energy Co. of New Orleans. Taylor and other independents are diverting capital from risky domestic exploration in order to buy working fields. Because their overhead expenses are lower, they expect to improve the economic production from these fields.

But this means that the independents are being pulled out of the exploration business. And independents traditionally have been the pioneers who have found new pools of oil and gas.

Indeed, the decline in U.S. oil and gas reserves and production and the corresponding increase in our dependence on foreign oil over the past decade is directly linked to the drop in the number of independent operators. Although noted earlier, it is worth repeating because the numbers are so alarming:

In 1983, a total of 12,892 "operators of record"—drillers in charge of overseeing an exploration project—were active in the United States. Only eight years later, by 1991, this number had dropped to 4,244—a decline of almost 70 percent! Similarly, new hydrocarbon reserves added by independent operators fell from 4.3 billion barrels of oil and liquid natural gas in 1983 to 1.5 billion barrels in 1991, a plunge of more than 65 percent. Thus, between 1983 and 1990 (data for 1991 were not available at the time this book was being written) capital expenditures for exploration and development of new fields by independent operators deteriorated by an alarming 60 percent, to less than $10 billion in 1990 from $22 billion only eight years before.[2]

Those numbers, which point toward the extinction of the independent U.S. oil and gas producer, are almost certain to worsen if the proposed rules governing contingency funds for "offshore" oil spills are adopted by Congress as written. Thus the first step toward protecting a vital domestic industry would be to junk the most abusive provisions of

OPA '90, as the Oil Pollution Act of 1990 is called. Few independents are able to reserve the $150 million in cash the 1990 law mandates to pay for cleaning up an offshore oil spill. And if they are unable to get insurance coverage for such a reserve—which is already happening— the only alternative will be to abandon their business or transfer their business overseas—which is also already happening.

The truth is that harsh tax laws and unreasonable restrictions on drilling, combined with punitive health and safety and environmental regulations, have made it impossible for many independent operators to stay in business. They are simply unable to raise the investment capital necessary to continue looking for new hydrocarbon reserves. For essentially the same reason it has been economically imprudent for major companies to seek new reserves of oil and gas in the United States.

While the oil and gas industry has been hit by harsh tax policies during the past decade, alternative fuels, for part of that time, have been encouraged by tax breaks. But, so far, no reasonably priced or popularly accepted alternative has been found to replace gasoline or diesel fuels. Replacing the automotive internal combustion engines driven by gasoline with vehicles fueled by natural gas, propane, or solar electric batteries will take decades, not years.

The energy situation in the United States has been exacerbated by an adversarial relationship between the energy industry and government. There seems to be a natural clash of ideas between people who work on the oil patch and those who staff a state or federal agency. Price regulations and production controls by government have sparked from most oil and gas producers an antagonism to political movements that have demanded environmental accountability, especially when some of these requirements were seen as unnecessary or excessive—at least in the eyes of the oil and gas producers. Government, moreover, has given little more than lip service to the threat posed by our dependence on foreign oil, and government bureaucrats have found it politically expedient to bow to consumers and environmentalists.

This has resulted in over-regulation of the industry. And current proposals threaten to make the regulatory burden even greater. It is hard to see the proposals without concluding that the ultimate consequences, if not objective, is to shut down the domestic oil industry.

(Natural gas is currently being favored as a replacement for oil. But when the coal and oil industries are stopped, the next target will be the domestic natural gas industry.)

A step in that direction was taken when environmentalists gained congressional support to ban exploration in huge areas of potentially oil-rich federal lands. The radical leadership of the environmental movement has accomplished this despite abundant evidence (and new technological developments, such as horizontal drilling) that can drill for oil and gas without significant dislocation to existing plant or animal life.

Yet another disincentive to exploring for other sources of oil and gas is the abundant supply of foreign oil, which is currently inexpensive and has lulled the nation into a false sense of security about the continued availability of cheap energy. After the collapse of oil prices in the 1980s, foreign energy has been tendered at relatively low prices.

But that price level is not what is usually meant by a "market-based" price. It is a price established and more or less maintained by the OPEC cartel. Periodically, OPEC loses control of production and prices fall. Periodically, the OPEC nations get together and agree to abide by production quotas and the price rises. One reason for the periodic "collapse of OPEC" and the fall in prices is that the OPEC nations need more cash flow. This need is made worse by the falling value of the U.S. dollar, since they sell oil for dollars. At any moment they can drop the price of oil worldwide simply by allowing production to increase—and their finding and production costs are dramatically lower than those in the United States. They are discouraged from taking this step for two reasons:

First, the OPEC nations desperately need the cash their oil resources provide. Without that money, their internal political stability is jeopardized. And, second, if they act in a clearly predatory way—that is, drop the price *for the purpose of driving U.S. competitors out of the market*—they risk retaliation from the United States. This also threatens their internal political stability.

The OPEC nations are obviously disadvantaged by increased production elsewhere in the world, including the United States. Thus, if from time to time, by accident or secret design, OPEC can "lose control" of its production quotas, overpump its oil, and drop its price for a time, it can weaken or bankrupt investors and drillers elsewhere, especially in high-cost areas such as the United States.

It is our belief that the losses of control that we have seen have been largely accidental. This despite what an unnamed Kuwaiti participant at a mid-1980s' OPEC meeting was quoted as saying—that the falling price of oil was having precisely the desired effect on other producers.

Whatever the case, this seemingly endless flow of oil has encouraged United States consumers mistakenly to believe that foreign suppliers can be counted on to continue providing petroleum for our consumption. This is where the matter of pricing enters the equation, and pricing is intimately related to the evaporation of domestic capital. By allowing foreign producers to dominate our oil supply, we have handed over control of the oil and gas market pricing mechanism to them. This might be acceptable, except for two basic problems.

First, as we've seen at least twice in the last two decades, foreign suppliers cannot be counted on to price energy in a manner consistent with U.S. consumer and industrial interests. Second, the market pricing mechanism is controlled overseas. Given U.S. tax and environmental regulations, U.S. producers have been unable to generate sufficient backing for new oil and gas exploration, development, and production, which might diminish that overseas control.

By all accounts, the United States has immense untapped oil fields. The U.S. Geological Survey estimates that as much as 70 billion barrels of oil and 507 trillion cubic feet of natural gas exist in fields that have not yet been drilled and, under current policies that restrict exploration on public lands, may never be.[3] Even so, we are still finding major new pools of oil and gas. In April 1993, for example, a joint venture by Arco and Phillips Petroleum Co. announced two new Alaskan discoveries containing almost 1.2 billion barrels of oil, and perhaps as much as 6 billion barrels.

Further, we need not rely only on new oil and gas discoveries to reduce our imports. Some geologists estimate that as much as *100 billion* more barrels of oil could be recovered from existing fields using new, more costly technologies. But at a market price of $20 a barrel, it makes no sense to recover this oil when it could cost at least that much to produce it.

There is a further dampener to seeking this oil—at any time OPEC could drop the world price well below $20 per barrel for an extended period. Potential investors must take into account how long they could survive if the price dropped. Thus, even if exploration and production drilling techniques could produce oil at $15, and even if the cost of getting it to market were $3, only a rank gambler would undertake the risk since even a modest drop in the price of oil could render the investment worthless. Moreover, most venture capital expects a reliable, early return on the investment.

Yet, despite the evidence of potentially large domestic oil and gas supplies—and alarming proof that the U.S. oil industry is on a downward slide toward disaster—federal policies continue to ignore or discourage domestic oil and gas exploration and production while trying to solve "the import problem" by cutting demand.

The most recent and obvious of these policies was the Clinton administration's failed proposal for a Btu tax on energy.

(Btu stands for "British thermal unit." It is a world standard for measuring the amount of heat produced by any source of energy. Basically, one Btu will raise the temperature of one pound of water by one degree. When you fill up with 10 gallons of unleaded at your neighborhood convenience store, for example, you are buying 1.25 million Btus of fuel.)

The Clinton Btu tax proposal was a stunningly bad idea. Even though it has foundered on the shoals of ineptitude, it, along with some of its permutations, is worth examining in some detail since it illustrates the Alice-in-Wonderland thinking that too often occurs in Washington, D.C., when energy is a primary issue. Concerning the Btu tax, industry associations were told by the administration that they would be punished unless they supported the Btu tax, and unions were given to understand that their hopes for administration backing of their "strikers' bill" depended on their support of the Clinton Btu tax. Few constituencies, as it turned out, liked the tax.

The idea of the Btu tax appears to have originated with the environmentalists who wanted a tax on carbon in the hopes that it would discourage the use of carbon-based fuels (coal, oil, natural gas, petroleum products). This objective was to be achieved regardless of the consequences to the economy—that is, to society. The carbon tax was shot dead in the water, primarily by Sen. Robert Byrd of West Virginia, a key coal state, who saw the proposal for what it was—a direct attack on coal.

The Clinton administration then got cute and proposed the Btu tax, which was nothing more than a carbon tax in disguise. Reduced to its essentials, the Clinton administration's Btu tax proposed to levy additional fees on fuel for each unit of energy the energy source produced. Initially, it sounded as if *all* energy sources would be taxed equally per Btu.

Not so. As proposed: renewables such as wind and solar were to be exempted; then, New England gained an exemption for heating oil (after a threat by Senate Majority Leader George Mitchell of Maine); then, different energy sources were to pay different amounts per Btu; then, petroleum products were to have been taxed at 59.9 cents per million Btus, except for some—such as gasoline used for agricultural production—which would not have been subject to any new taxes at all; then, primary aluminum production was exempted; then . . .

As the *New York Times* reported on June 2, 1993: "What resulted, some experts say, is one of the most exemption-loaded, head-scratchingly complicated, brow-furrowing revenue raisers in history. Never very simple, the proposed energy tax is now so convoluted that one fuel, diesel, would be taxed at at least five separate rates and dyed in enough distinguishing colors to make Crayola green with envy. [The tax would be based on the color of diesel fuel, which would be dyed according to its use.]

"In the House version of the bill, oil is taxed more than gas. Gas is taxed more than solar energy, which is not taxed at all. Electricity is taxed, but at a floating rate derived from the taxes on all the coal, oil, gas and other energy sources used to generate the previous month's power. . . .

"It is the first tax proposal to grant specific exemptions not just to certain molecules, but to one subatomic particle, the electron [which is essential to processing aluminum]."

It then turned out that the Btu tax would do little to raise net revenues or to reduce the deficit. The Clinton administration itself estimated that the Btu tax would raise only about $22–$25 billion annually. But private studies indicate that the tax would have cost the national economy as much as $40 billion a year—and $25 billion at a minimum, or more than the Btu tax would raise—in lost production by energy-intensive industries such as primary metals (iron, steel, aluminum) and agriculture. It makes no sense to throw a $25–40 billion monkey wrench into the economy in an effort to raise $22–25 billion in tax revenues.

As an environmentally correct social measure, the Btu tax was considered a penalty on "dirty" energy, and thus an encouragement to use so-called "clean" fuels. It was, quite simply, a clumsy effort to use taxation to implement social policies rather than to raise public revenues to finance social improvements. But in this respect, too, the plan was a dismal failure, among other reasons because such "clean" fuels as natural gas and hydroelectric power would be taxed at the same rate as coal.

The flaws of the Btu tax fell over one another. Where the oil and gas industry was directly concerned, the original Btu tax on natural gas would have been levied at the wellhead, which would have created a serious problem for the industry. Adding even as little as 25 cents per thousand cubic feet of gas, the estimated tax would have been enough to sink producers locked into long-term utility contracts set at $1.90 per thousand cubic feet or less. This would have meant even less "clean" natural gas available for consumption, not to mention more lost jobs and production capacity in the oil patch.

But the heaviest burden from the tax, as initially proposed, would have fallen on consumers least able to afford it. The White House itself estimated that the average family of four would have paid $320 more each year for electricity, home heating oil, and gasoline. Nor does this take into account the incremental energy costs in virtually every other commodity a family of four requires for existence—food, clothing, and other basics.

In our opinion, the Clinton administration's Btu tax proposal would have sacrificed an entire layer of people at the bottom of the economic pyramid in order to accomplish social and environmental goals. And these would not even have been achieved!

Finally, and fascinatingly, while administration estimates showed almost no change in consumption as a result of the Btu tax, the proposed Btu tax was a source of great annoyance to our OPEC allies. They might even have retaliated by reducing the flow of energy exports, raising prices, or a combination of the two.

In mid-April 1993, the oil ministers of twenty-five OPEC and other producing nations met in Muscat, Oman, to protest the proposed Btu tax, which would have added about $3.50 to the price of a barrel of oil—about 17.5 percent above the prevailing $20 level. "We are serious about not wanting these taxes," said OPEC president Alirio Parra of Venezuela, apparently fearing that the tax would reduce consumption. The meeting ended with a not-so-veiled threat of retaliation. According to the *New York Times*, a communiqué issued after the session said prices were already too low and "a new wave of tax increases *which are discriminatory against oil*" would have a destabilizing effect on the oil industry (emphasis added). OPEC and other producing nations, said the communiqué, will examine "options open to them, to mitigate the impacts on their economies."

Again, on June 29, 1993, in a speech in Washington, D.C., Dr. Subroto, secretary general of OPEC, took up the energy tax proposals in the consuming countries. Pointing out that OPEC members have continually called for more cooperation among producers, consumers, and the international oil industry, he warned, "This does not mean that consumer governments can dismiss the possibility that the producers might take action" if already high energy taxes are raised further.

Dr. Subroto added that the producers felt their livelihoods would be at stake if oil were taxed further and consumption lowered. Should the carbon tax being considered in the European Community be adopted, he said, "the call on OPEC oil would fall by 2.5 million barrels a day by the year 2010." OPEC would then have to cut back on planned production expansion and risk a world energy shortage, price hikes, and market instability.[4]

And since the world oil pricing apparatus *rests entirely outside the United States*, the price we pay for oil is almost entirely at the mercy of foreign suppliers. This will continue to be the case so long as we import a high and increasing percentage of our oil.

It is our belief that an aggressive program to stimulate U.S. production would find and produce more oil than most experts predict, and that such a program and the resulting increase in domestic production would have a sobering impact on foreign producers. We suggest that foreign producers would be less inclined to attempt any kind of power play with oil supply or prices if the U.S. followed an aggressive policy of oil exploration and development at home.

A number of policies and programs should be instituted to stimulate investment in domestic U.S. exploration and production, and thereby reduce our political, economic, and social vulnerability to foreign manipulation. These include:

1. Imposing an oil import security premium—not a conventional tariff, but a measure that would establish a floor that would prevent a collapse of oil prices within the United States
2. Removing completely the alternative minimum tax on domestic oil and gas exploration, development, and production companies
3. Restoring an oil depletion allowance that provides for the reinvestment of the funds generated in exploration and development activities
4. Opening up for oil and gas exploration and development all promising federally owned lands
5. Stop imposing new costly environmental regulations on the oil and gas industry, and develop a mechanism for weighing the economic impact and scientific validity of environmental restrictions. (This mechanism should apply across the board, and not only to the oil and gas industry.)

Before looking at these suggestions in more detail, we should note that a clear signal from our government that it recognized the importance of this basic industry and that, as a matter of public policy, it wanted to encourage its renewed vitality would be as important as any of the above proposals.

1. An oil import security premium.
For nearly two decades there have been proposals, usually from somewhere in the oil patch, to institute a tariff on imported oil. A tariff—a tax on imported goods—may be levied in a number of ways.

Ordinarily, it is a fixed amount on each unit of an imported product, or a fixed percentage of the value or price of the product.

Such a conventional tariff on imported oil would have at least two major flaws. First, it would add to the price of oil products, exactly as would the Clinton administration's Btu tax proposal, with all of the harmful effects described earlier. And second, a conventional tariff on imported petroleum products would lead to an entirely new panoply of destructive government rules, regulations, and penalty taxes similar to those imposed in the 1970s. It might require an entirely new federal bureaucracy to implement it. We need simplicity, not complexity.

What we propose would be so different from an ordinary tariff that we have chosen to identify it with a different name.

First, the title, "security premium," is intended to suggest an insurance-type concept which would be in the interest of the nation. And that is precisely what we intend—that it provide protection for our overall national energy supplies.

Second, in certain limited circumstances—such as a temporary decline in the price of oil—an import security premium would operate to slow the price fall by simply adding an amount to the price of oil and gas products as they are brought into the United States from other countries. Since the U.S. government already collects a customs fee of a few cents a barrel, the mechanism is already in place. All that needs to be determined is the amount of the premium.

Third, an import security premium could be structured so that it would not be added to the prevailing price of oil at the time the premium was imposed. It would not, as some have suggested, be an addition of, say, $5 a barrel. For $20 a barrel, this would immediately add 20 percent to prices and have the same damaging impact on domestic industrial production and consumer prices as would the failed Btu tax. While a sustained boost in worldwide prices would benefit the domestic oil and gas exploration and production industry, the rest of our economy would suffer.

Yet our vulnerability to price crashes, *whether predatory or unintentional*, ought to be eradicated. Since, as noted earlier, foreign producers control the market price of oil, they can ravage the domestic U.S. petroleum industry.

How, then, would an import security premium avoid the pitfalls of a tariff, and at the same time avoid the threat to our domestic industry of potentially predatory pricing practices by foreign producers? In order to accomplish these objectives, certain principles should be adhered to.

First, to repeat, no import security premium should be imposed if it raises the current base price of oil.

Second, nothing should be done that requires the creation of a new federal bureaucracy or collection mechanism.

Third, no fee should be imposed solely for the purpose of raising revenue for the federal government. If a fee is levied to generate revenues, then it likely would become a permanent tax. An import security premium should not be permanent.

Fourth, no fee should be imposed solely for the purpose of protecting a fundamentally uncompetitive U.S. industry. We believe that the U.S. oil industry is perfectly capable of competing in a world market provided it is not subject to arbitrary, possibly predatory, short-term price collapses that destroy investment incentive and the like. We do not believe that the long-term price of oil will be less than $20 a barrel, or thereabouts despite a downward drift in the last half of 1993. As our proposal will show, if the world price of oil drops below $20 for an extended period of time, what some might call "permanently," our proposal for an ISP would require U.S. industry to compete in that long-term market.

Fifth, any fee that is imposed ought to relate in some way to an appropriate objective; that is, there should be some rationale for collecting a fee other than protectionism or raising revenue. Then, if that objective (for example, paying for the Strategic Petroleum Reserve) is ever met, the fee could be terminated. (We wish to avoid creating a fee that would continue when the reason for it no longer exists.)

Instead of adding to the price of oil with a direct import fee, we believe an import security premium should guarantee that if the world price of oil drops, that price reduction would not pass through immediately to the U.S. market. It would not be so much a fee as a floor under the price of oil.

There is almost no limit to the ways in which an import security premium could operate. Here is one example of how the floor might work:

Suppose that at the time the floor is imposed, the world price of oil is $20 a barrel. (Since there is no such thing as a single world price of oil—oil comes in a vast array of qualities and grades, and the price of each is different—the floor could readily be established for each grade of petroleum product.) The floor price could be set at $20 the barrel or at $1 below the then-world price. For simplicity's sake, we will set it at $20.

If, subsequent to establishing the floor price, the world price should drop by 10 cents per barrel, the floor would require that the U.S. government collect an additional 10 cents on each barrel of imported oil. If the price dropped 50 cents per barrel, the import security premium would be 50 cents per barrel, and so on for each decline in price.

Consider the effect. The world price would probably not drop below $20 per barrel, because foreign suppliers would recognize that if they cut prices, the lost revenues would go to the U.S. government. But if the price did fall below $20 for a short period of time, our domestic oil and gas industry would not suffer—drilling rigs would not shut down, investors would not lose their capital, oil would not be locked up and lost forever—because competitive imported oil would continue to sell for $20 a barrel inside the United States. Consumers would not get the benefit of a price reduction, but they might not anyway, for experience shows that minor, temporary fluctuations do not have much effect on gasoline prices.

Suppose further that despite the floor, over time, oil continues to be significantly overproduced elsewhere in the world. That could occur for any number of reasons. Beyond the use of oil as a weapon against the United States, three possible causes could be: a miscalculation of market demand; a worldwide economic downturn that would reduce overall oil consumption; a price war initiated by one foreign producer to drive other foreign competitors out of business or increase market share.

But let us assume that the world price drop is not temporary. It continues for several months and the price drops each month by $1 per barrel. After five months, the price would be $15 per barrel. It could stabilize and hold there for several months; it could continue to drop; or it could begin to rise.

In such a situation, our proposed floor should not remain at $20 per barrel permanently. This would disadvantage American industry as it tries to compete in global markets with foreign manufacturers. But if history is any indication, foreign competitors, at least in the European community, would also be seeing higher taxes on oil, although some or all of these would eventually be rebated.

Thus the floor in such a price plunge should slowly move in the direction of the price decline. For example, after three months the floor would drop by 5 percent of the difference between the original floor ($20) and the price at the end of the third month ($17), namely, $3 × .05 = $0.15. The new floor would be $19.85. (The selection of 5 percent is, of course, arbitrary.) The objective is to avoid following the world price too rapidly; this would discourage anyone from using a price cut to damage the U.S. domestic industry.

At the end of the fourth month, the price has dropped to $16.00. The difference from the original floor is $4; thus the floor price would drop by 5 percent of $4—i.e., by $0.20 to $19.65.

At the end of the fifth month, the price has dropped to $15.00. The difference from the original floor is $5; thus the floor price would drop by 5 percent—i.e., by $0.25 to $19.40.

If the world price held at $15 for many months, the floor would continue to drop at the rate of 5 percent of the difference between the original floor price of $20 and the world price at the end of the month, until the new floor price reached a level $1.00 above the world price. At that point the new floor would hold until the world price either dropped further, or began to rise. The reason for holding at a level above the world price is that the day-to-day fluctuations over the course of the month could exceed that difference.

During the time that the world price was below the floor price of the ISP, the U.S. government would collect revenues based on the difference between the floor price and the world price. Thus, using the example we have been discussing, the prices and ISP collections would look like this:*

---

* We have vastly oversimplified this example for purposes of discussion and illustration. Our example assumes that the price drops $1.00 on the first day of the month and holds steady for the entire month. At this point, on the first day of the next month, it drops another $1.00; and so on.

MONTH	FLOOR PRICE	WORLD PRICE	ISP
1	$20.00	$19.00	$1.00
2	$20.00	$18.00	$2.00
3	$20.00	$17.00	$3.00
4	$19.85	$16.00	$3.85
5	$19.65	$15.00	$4.65
6	$19.40	$15.00	$4.40
7	$19.15	$15.00	$4.15
8	$18.90	$15.00	$3.90
9	$18.65	$15.00	$3.65
10	$18.40	$15.00	$3.40
***			
15	$17.15	$15.00	$2.15
***			
19	$16.15	$15.00	$1.15
20	$16.00	$15.00	$1.00

As the world price would begin to rise, the floor would similarly climb each month until it again reached $20. There are numerous ways of doing this. As just one example, it would be possible to have the floor "follow" the world price upward once the world price reached and then exceeded the floor price:

MONTH	FLOOR PRICE	WORLD PRICE	ISP
21	$16.00	$16.00	$0.00
22	$16.00	$16.50	$0.00
23	$16.50	$17.00	$0.00
24	$17.00	$18.00	$0.00
25	$18.00	$20.00	$0.00
26	$20.00	$20.50	$0.00
27	$20.00	$20.50	$0.00

Part of the rationale behind this proposal is that if the producing countries were confronted by a floor on the U.S. import price, world prices would probably not drop below that level and, if they did, they would not remain below $20 for very long. Further, by dropping the floor slowly toward the world price during a period of oil-market decline, some of the benefits would be passed along to consumers and American industry. The longer the price remained down, the narrower the gap between world prices and U.S. prices.

Another part of the rationale for the ISP is that we do not believe that price drops below $20 per barrel, or something in that range, are "real"—that they will be sustained for any length of time. Whether by accident or design, such price drops will shut down U.S. production (and any other high cost production in the world). Once that has happened, the price will not only go back up to $20, but higher. Any gains realized by our economy from the temporary price drop will rapidly be neutralized by increased prices, lost wages and taxes, adverse balance of trade, and the like. In what we believe to be the unlikely event that a long-term price decline should occur, the fact that the price floor would follow it slowly downward would keep our energy supply from being badly overpriced over the long haul.

Further, establishing an oil price should not upset OPEC (nor should we allow OPEC to dictate our domestic policies). Such a floor would not reduce oil consumption unlike a tax or a tariff, which would add an amount to the existing world price of oil. The main impact of the floor would be to remove the temptation to engage in predatory pricing in order to force out competition. If any foreign producer should object to the ISP, it would suggest an intention to do just that— to engage in price cutting in order to drive U.S. domestic producers out of business. Such objections would only emphasize our need to defend our domestic oil and gas industry. Without a floor price, that industry is totally vulnerable.

Confronted by such a policy by the United States—the world's largest consumer of petroleum products—foreign producers would probably do everything possible to restore the world price to at least $20 as quickly as possible.

A floor would also tend to prevent artificial price cuts, just as the mere existence of the U.S. Strategic Petroleum Reserve has helped reduce speculation-driven price fluctuations in world oil prices. Such a program would allow American investors to drill domestic fields and build production facilities with some confidence that sharply declining prices would not wipe them out.

The history of the oil business tells us that there would be some continued risk of a long-term downturn in prices, but a small risk because foreign oil-producing nations could not afford very long periods of drastically reduced income.

Five additional facets of this proposal require some discussion:

- *The way the floor price is first established.*

The floor price for each grade of oil would be based on the seasonally adjusted price of that grade of oil over the prior three months but in no event higher than the price at the time the floor is established. It is important that both absolute prices and seasonally adjusted price levels be taken into account since there are annual fluctuations in the price of petroleum products between seasons. Home heating oil, for example, generally rises in price during winter months when seasonal demand is strong. Unleaded gasoline prices tend to rise during summer vacation driving peaks. Economists can level seasonal swings by calculating how much the time of year affects price levels for specific grades of petroleum products. As an alternative to the calculation of seasonal effects, the period for the price rise necessary to raise the floor could be extended to nine or twelve months.

Any other approach to provide a reasonable approximation of world prices could be used. But one requirement is important: however established, the price set for the floor should not be higher than the price on the day the price floor is fixed. Thus, consumers would not experience a price increase as a result of the floor.

- *The way the floor would be adjusted upward over time if world prices begin a long-term rise.*

We have described how the floor would work if world oil prices dropped. But what would happen if prices increased over a long period of time?

Suppose that a year after the price floor is set the world price has inched upward to $21 per barrel. We would propose that the floor should be elevated to mirror what would appear to have become a new, higher, stable world price. As a suggestion, every time the seasonally adjusted world price rises 5 percent or more above the floor (in this example, to $21 a barrel) and maintains that level for three months, the floor would rise by 2.5 percent, or 50 cents, to $20.50. With the new floor at $20.50, if the world price rose to or above $21.525 per barrel, or another 5 percent above the floor, and stayed there for three months, the floor would rise by 2.5 percent to 21.01 dollars.

The effect of this increase in the floor would be to reflect actual increases in world oil prices, but not short-term price volatility. During these times the domestic industry would be able to sell its oil at or near the world price. The only effect of raising the floor price would be to provide a new level to which imports would be held so that our domestic industry would not suffer from sudden, short-term attacks by foreign producers.

• *How the Import Security Premium would be imposed.*

The first purchaser inside the United States would be required to report the price of the purchase delivered to a point at the border or within the country and pay the ISP. This would eliminate the problem of attempting to "tax" shippers or producers outside the United States.

• *The use of revenues, if any, produced by the floor.*

The effect of a floor at $20 would be to stabilize world oil prices at or above $20 per barrel. Some economists, and many independent producers, might argue that this is not a level sufficient to encourage renewed domestic production, that a more reasonable figure is $25 or $30 per barrel. For producers operating at marginally profitable levels, this argument has validity.

But most of the weak exploration and production companies have already fallen out, and the remainder are making around $20 a barrel. The purpose of an ISP should be to establish a price level below which the price will not rapidly fall, not a high average that would attract speculators to leap back into the oil patch as they did in response to unrealistically high prices in the late 1970s and early 1980s.

In any event, a floor at $20 per barrel would not bring about the collection of an import security premium unless the long-term world price dropped below $20 per barrel, which, as we have said and history demonstrates, is an unlikely event. But if any revenues did accrue they should be applied to the nation's Strategic Petroleum Reserve Account (actually, the general fund of the U.S. Treasury), which at $20 per barrel had a value of about $11.4 billion at the end of 1991. Interestingly, the example used earlier of the ISP consequences should the world price fall to $15 for twenty months, would be some $13.9 billion. It seems inconceivable that foreign producers would overproduce oil in a way to permit the U.S. government to collect such revenues.

Incidentally, the cost of the Strategic Petroleum Reserve for oil, equipment, and interest exceeded $25 billion in 1985, and by now very likely is more than *$40 billion*. These sums have been paid by taxpayers. Meanwhile, consumers of petroleum products have profited from the "insurance" provided by the Strategic Petroleum Reserve without paying the premiums when gasoline is bought. These "premiums" are part of the cost of our protection from overdependency on imported oil. The fact is that America's taxpayers have paid to build a reserve that can provide a shield against an interruption of supply of imported oil.[5] Any money collected from establishing a floor price for imports should go to pay off that account.

It is as inconceivable that the United States could ever completely eliminate its use of imported oil as it is that enough money could ever be collected to pay off the cost, plus interest, of the Strategic Petroleum Reserve. But if this should happen, we would recommend that the entire import-security premium approach be reexamined. In doing so, we would be recognizing that the floor must not be considered as a means of raising revenue for the government—in short, that it is not a tax. Taxing energy, as we have argued, is a bad idea. The purpose of an import security premium is entirely different. It should be limited to collecting the amounts necessary to pay for the Strategic Petroleum Reserve.

• *The duration of the floor.*
Assuming, as we do, that the revenues would never be sufficient to pay for the Strategic Petroleum Reserve, it would seem appropriate to provide that the floor be terminated fifteen years after being established, unless a policy debate should result in a decision to extend it. Thus any investments made, jobs created, fields developed, or improvements gained in the oil patch during the life of the floor would be safe from predatory pricing by overseas producers. Once we were within three years or so of the end of the floor, a decision could be made primarily on economic grounds whether to continue to encourage domestic drilling

with an import security premium. A principal reason for suggesting a time limit is that in today's world, it is unreasonable to expect that any system will still be appropriate after fifteen years. And unless the termination is provided when the floor is established, it will be very hard to change, much less end, even if it becomes useless or, worse, counterproductive due to altered market conditions, new technologies, a change in the balance of international political power, or other developments that influence the complexities of the global energy industry.

2. Removing completely the alternative minimum tax on domestic oil and gas exploration, development, and production companies.

Clearly, the structure of taxes levied on the petroleum industry is discriminatory. The industry is taxed not only to raise revenues at all levels of government, but also to penalize it for past misbehavior—sometimes real, more often imagined—and because of suspicions about the industry's future conduct.

The energy industry, for its part, distrusts the government acutely. An example of why the industry has become wary of the federal government's taxing policies came shortly before the end of the Bush administration. In one of the final tax bills passed by Congress, the Bush administration proposed, and Congress agreed, to allow a reduction in the alternative minimum tax on oil and gas producers. As chapter 3 explained, the alternative minimum tax imposed by the 1986 Tax Reform Act meant that many producers were required to pay cash taxes even if they had no cash earnings to meet the tax obligation because the AMT disallowed certain "intangible" drilling expenses as legitimate tax deductions. That meant that even though these "intangible" expenses included such essential services as geological surveys, if your actual income taxes were lower and if you could not deduct "intangible" costs, you had to pay a higher tax as an "alternative minimum."

The AMT has been a painful and costly burden for oil exploration companies, with not much hope of its removal at the time of this writing. Since the Clinton administration, with superenvironmentalist Al Gore as vice president, has given no signal of how much, when, or even if the alternative minimum tax would be reduced, there has been no rush to resume exploratory drilling.

An indication of the industry's skepticism was provided by the weekly rig count during the first three months of 1993, when relief from the AMT was supposed to be forthcoming under the Bush proposal as passed by Congress. If the industry had believed it was going to get a tax break, exploration and production companies would presumably have begun leasing additional rigs and getting them into operation. But the Baker Hughes U.S. rig count actually *declined* to 611 rigs in March 1993, when the AMT burden was meant to be relieved, from 648 rigs in March 1992, when no AMT relief was in sight.[6]

An immediate step—one that might have as much psychological impact as financial impact—would be to eliminate the alternative minimum tax for all oil and gas producers, and to do so at once.

3. Restoring an oil depletion allowance that provides for reinvestment in exploration and development activities.

A second, and far more important, tax proposal would be to restore the oil depletion allowance for domestic production. As reported in chapter 3, this tax "incentive" initially was granted to the oil and gas industry in recognition of the fact that the sale of oil involved the depletion of a capital asset. The producer needed cash to find additional oil to replace the depleted value of the assets that had been sold to satisfy consumer demands. But in 1960, Congress began nibbling away at the depletion allowance—which critics viewed as a loophole rather than a legitimate economic fact of the oil and gas business—and in 1975 virtually removed it.

One reason for this development, of course, was that oil prices were rising sharply due to the Arab oil embargo, and domestic producers were accused of gouging U.S. consumers and making outrageous profits rather than using the oil depletion allowance to look for new hydrocarbon deposits. So it made political sense, even if the economic logic was based on false premises, to "punish" oil producers for rising prices.

A simple way to avoid having an oil-depletion allowance "misused" would be to allow the tax advantage only for the amount of money a producer put into new exploration and production ventures. If a producer pocketed the profits or distributed those profits to shareholders as dividends, then he or she would get no tax break on depleting irreplaceable (or, more accurately, unreplaced) assets. This would encourage producers to look for new oil and gas in the United States, and in our opinion it would generate much more in revenues for the federal government from taxes and from unemployment cost-savings than it would cost.

4. Opening up for oil and gas exploration and development all promising federally owned land.

An import security fee, or floor, would provide protection to producers from unfair foreign competition and predatory price wars. Total elimination of the alternative minimum tax would give the industry economic and psychological encouragement to reenter the oil patch. Restoration of the oil depletion allowance would furnish the financial incentive necessary to attract new capital for oil and gas exploration and development. But once all this is accomplished, where would independents and majors begin looking for new oil and gas? Unless lands and waters which are presently off limits are made available for exploration, they would have to do more intense drilling in areas already substantially drilled.

The most favorable area is a small portion of the Arctic National Wildlife Reserve (ANWR). This area, which Congress recognized in section 1002 of the act creating ANWR, and its petroleum-deposit potential were thoroughly discussed in chapter 5. But herewith a brief summary to explain what can be done to rescue the American oil patch.

A part of the Arctic National Wildlife Reserve coastal plain, the "1002" area, where most of the oil and gas deposits are believed to be, encompasses about 1.5 million acres of almost entirely uninhabited land out of the 19 million acres of ANWR. To put some numbers in perspective, begin with the potential oil and gas deposits.

According to government studies, there is at least a 50–50 chance of finding as much as 9.2 billion barrels of oil in this area, and more optimistic estimates indicate that the deposits could hold as much as 15 to 30 billion barrels.[7] Yet, environmentalists are almost fanatically keeping the Arctic National Wildlife Reserve from oil and gas exploration and production. Given the small size of the area that would be affected, what damage would be done to the environment by searching for new hydrocarbon deposits?

Before answering, remember that exploration and development of the North Slope fields around Prudhoe Bay had no lasting negative impact on the delicate environment of the region. The caribou herd has actually increased more than sixfold since oil companies completed the Trans-Alaska Pipeline and put production in place.

This is an important point, because oilfield technology has made dramatic advances since the first half of the 1970s when drilling commenced at the North Slope fields. In terms of developing potential deposits beneath the Arctic National Wildlife Reserve, the most important of these advances is a technique known as "directional" drilling. This is a procedure whereby vertical drills are thrust deeply into the earth, and then slanted laterally toward geological formations that have been identified by prior studies as probably containing oil and gas deposits. The result is one drill-stem hole that angles outward in one of several directions, rather than several drill bits punching vertical holes at numerous sites.

Thus it would be possible for exploration rigs to use a thirteen thousand-acre area of the ANWR coastal plain as a platform to drill for oil beneath 1.5 million adjacent acres of land. This topography, scattered in individual tracts throughout the 13,000 acres, would support roads, platforms, buildings, and small drilling pads, each of which could handle up to eighteen wells drilled directionally out of the main hole. It could be accomplished without seriously disturbing either the flora, fauna, or natural habitat of any creatures, or the existence of the few humans to live, hunt, or fish the region.

While the Arctic National Wildlife Reserve is the most promising of the potentially rich domestic oilfield deposits, it is by no means the only one. Much of the land owned by the federal government in the western United States, with potentially rich deposits, has also been placed off-limits to exploratory drilling. Environmental restrictions have put a bar on *any* development, even development based upon new technologies that, by any reasonable interpretation, pose no environmental dangers. If exploration were to be allowed in these areas, it would be governed by stringent protective environmental regulations.

According to the U.S. Department of Energy, since 1859 about 161.5 billion barrels of oil and 800.4 trillion cubic feet of natural gas have been pumped from fields in the United States. About 20 percent of the oil and 37 percent of the natural gas has come from areas owned by the federal government and leased to private producers who, by the way, paid royalties of 16.67 percent of gross revenues to the federal Treasury.[8]

More importantly, however, although the 1990 U.S. proved reserves of oil were 26.3 billion barrels, the USGS has estimated that there are 189 billion barrels of oil and 978 trillion cubic feet of natural gas still to be produced in the United States at today's prices and with today's technologies. Much of this oil and gas is projected to be on federal land and under federal waters. Numbers such as these (by no means the highest estimates available) suggest that with sufficient will and commitment, the United States could become a great deal more self-sufficient in oil and gas than generally thought.

But today, almost a third of the federally-owned lands have been placed on a list of publicly owned properties that cannot be explored for new oil and gas production. In consequence, the ultimate recovery from existing U.S. oil and gas fields is much lower than the 189 billion barrels of oil and 978 trillion cubic feet of gas estimated by the U.S. Department of Energy at the end of 1991. Absent a thorough geological survey of these areas, many of which have been placed off-limits, it is almost impossible to determine how much oil and gas will remain untapped under existing prohibitions. But even if it is as little as 30 percent of the Department of Energy estimate of 189 billion barrels, it would represent about 63 billion barrels of oil. That translates to almost 9 million barrels of production a day for twenty years, without resorting to exotic production techniques that are both technologically more difficult and economically more expensive.

Put another way, at $20 per barrel, $180 million a day, about $60 billion a year, would be contributed to our domestic economy rather than to foreign suppliers.

5. Stop imposing new costly environmental regulations on the oil and gas industry.

A final environmental issue is additional regulation. This was noted in chapter 4.

To propose including oil-field materials as hazardous wastes is, in effect, to apply regulations for growing apples to those that govern growing oranges. Petroleum exploration and production waste byproducts are not the same as those produced by other industries. For example, underground disposal of water that is a byproduct of drilling for oil and gas is a very expensive proposition already required by the state of Louisiana and under consideration by the federal government. Such a requirement is reasonable if a small body of water is significantly affected by a foreign discharge. But in the Gulf of Mexico, with its many currents and mixings and volumes of water, it is unreasonable to prohibit mixing in small amounts of drilling-byproduct water that might be slightly more saline than the Gulf water.

What is needed is a new cooperative relationship between government and the oil and gas industry to review existing environmental regulations to determine which make sense and should be continued, and which do not make sense in light of current scientific knowledge. What is *not* needed are new and costly burdens on an essential industry that desperately needs help to survive for the benefit of the nation's economy, population, political strength, and social resilience.

This cooperative effort should begin with a determination to make environmental decisions on the basis of economic *and* environmental cost-benefit analyses rather than sound bites or film clips that dwell upon emotionally charged images of caribou, seals, or wildflowers. The U.S. energy industry led the world in demonstrating that it can survive and prosper in harmony with the environment. Let society in general try to understand the realities of the oil and gas industry. To do so is in the best interests of all of us.

It would be extremely helpful to establish a good-faith, working relationship between the energy industry and government. Such a relationship would improve the chances of supplying the nation with adequate hydrocarbon supplies and thus minimize the impact of foreign interference in our economy and lifestyle.

The crisis in the oil patch is real and it is urgent. Solving the crisis will not totally resolve the problem of dependence on foreign energy. At our current and projected rates of energy consumption, we will always need large amounts of foreign oil and gas.

Nor will solving the current crisis in the oil patch be a permanent solution to America and the world's energy future. That can come only when alternative supplies of energy—nuclear, solar, wind, water, geothermal, biomass, ocean thermal gradients, and perhaps even "breakthrough" technologies beyond our current imagination—become affordable for all of our energy needs. The gleam in the eye of creative energy inventors might one day be the little black box in every house and office that will supply all of mankind's energy needs cleanly, inexpensively, and efficiently.

Can it be done? Who knows? But it hasn't happened yet.

Every domestic energy source, not just domestic oil production, is held hostage to the threat of a dramatic world oil price collapse. Alternative sources of energy, just like domestic oil supplies, can only be developed if they can attract capital investment. Unless predatory pricing from outside the United States, intentional or not, can be controlled, investment in energy alternatives will remain on the fringe.

For the moment, the crisis in America's oil patch is immediate. Easing that crisis—one that has been created by shortsighted policies and special-interest politics—can contribute greatly to supplying not just our own but the world's energy needs for ten or twenty or maybe even fifty future generations.

Our nation's oil and gas supplies can also create domestic wealth while we wait for that little black box. If low-cost alternatives to hydrocarbons are eventually developed, the oil and gas that has not been produced will be locked in forever, without having conferred its wealth on our national economy and society.

All of these are good reasons. But there is another.

America's leadership in global energy development has not been limited to its oil and gas reserves. More recently, that leadership has been demonstrated in the development of hydrocarbon-alternative fuels. One reason for the strength of that leadership has been the vitality of our economy. And our economy—as well as our prosperity and social fabric—is placed in grave jeopardy by relying too heavily on foreign oil supplies, as we have done and are still doing.

The simple truth is: Reviving America's oil patch is essential if we are to avoid economic, political, and social upheavals before we have an opportunity to move from the Age of Hydrocarbons to a new, more technologically progressive, politically sane, and environmentally responsible future.

AFTERWORD

In April 1993 two diverse incidents illustrated something about the wondrous complexities of nature's gift of hydrocarbon deposits to mankind.

In Alaska, where the North Slope fields have proven to be a bounteous storehouse of energy wealth for the United States, two petroleum companies announced finding new fields of oil and gas that contained almost 2 billion barrels of oil, perhaps as much as 6 billion barrels. They were not on the North Slope. They were in Cook Inlet, where until then some critics of the oil and gas industry had said (probably wishful thinking) that no significant hydrocarbon energy was to be found.

The Cook Inlet discovery, even at its minimally estimated size, is more than twice the size of the nation's Strategic Petroleum Reserve. And, as it is brought to market over the next ten to twenty years, it will provide hundreds of thousands of barrels of oil each day, thus reducing our dependence on imports by an equivalent amount. The announcement was a modestly important business story, but seemingly of little consequence since Americans expect their oil companies to find and produce the oil we have come to accept as a right fundamental to our lifestyle.

During the same month an excavating company boring a subway hole through the soft Austin Chalk formation near downtown Dallas hit upon a pocket of methane gas that suspended construction for a couple of days until the volatile fumes could be exhausted with fans and construction crews safely resume their labors.

In contrast to the major Alaskan find, the methane gas deposit made page one news in many communities because it was such a curiosity. For one thing, Dallas is not a center of oil and gas production, despite the popular image conveyed by television. No commercially exploitable hydrocarbon deposits have ever been found within fifty miles of the city.

More important to some news-gathering organizations was the geological discovery reported by the subway tunneling project. Million of years ago, the waters of the Gulf of Mexico extended to about where downtown Dallas is today. The first explanation of the methane gas deposit was that in the distant past, a large colony of seaworms chose a shoreside site to feed, reproduce, and die. As they were covered by silt and sand and other rocks that eventually created the Austin Chalk formation, the seaworms decomposed and, through the marvel of nature, were miraculously transformed and became a gas deposit awaiting exposure when that drill bit of a subway tunneling machine found them 60 million years later. More sophisticated geological analyses were then conducted. And these determined that a possibility existed—slight, to be sure, but a possibility nonetheless—that the methane gas was an upward seepage from a potentially large hydrocarbon field that lay perhaps ten thousand feet or more beneath the Austin Chalk formation where no oil and gas could possibly exist, according to all previous geological evidence.

These incidents illustrate a basic truth: Nature has endowed mankind with so many diverse types of hydrocarbon and other potential energy fuels in so many different places that their mere discovery is a cause for wonder as well as celebration. These are gifts that we have used in glorious ways to enrich our lives and bring peace and stability to the world, and to fight wars that we believed as a matter of national policy to be just and necessary.

America's oil-patch wealth is not a staple that should lie unused beneath the surface of the earth, not when it can bring so many benefits to the nation and to the world.

That is why America's oil patch must be saved from the destruction it surely faces unless the nation reverses the devastating energy policies it has followed for more than a decade. The issue is not "use it or lose it." The issue is this: If our government will free this tremendously energetic industry from unnecessary, burdensome, and foolish restraints, it will again contribute enormously to America's—and the world's— continuous search for a better, more productive, and more fulfilling life.

ENDNOTES

FOREWORD

1. New York, N.Y.: Simon & Schuster, 1991. *THE PRIZE* won the 1992 Pulitzer Prize for nonfiction.
2. Other industrialized nations' nuclear-power generation in 1991, as a percentage of electricity produced, were: Sweden, 40 percent; Germany, 27.6 percent; Japan, 23.8 percent; the former USSR, 12.8 percent; and Canada, 16.4 percent. Source: International Atomic Energy Agency.

CHAPTER 1

1. *World Oil Trends*, 1991 edition, Cambridge Energy Research Associates and Arthur Anderson & Co., Cambridge, Mass.
2. Ibid., Table 1, p. 6.
3. *Petroleum Independent*, published by the Independent Petroleum Association of America, Vol. 62, No. 7, p. 10, Washington, D.C. (September 1992).
4. *Fortune* magazine, April 22, 1991, p. 144.
5. Statistical Abstract of the United States, 1992, Table 645, p. 405, Bureau of the Census, U.S. Department of Commerce, Government Printing Office, Washington, D.C. (1992).
6. Ibid.
7. *Fortune*, op. cit., p. 142.
8. An "operator of record" is the company responsible to regulators for drilling a well. These represent only part of the total number of independent operators. For example, three companies may jointly drill a well, but only one is listed as the "operator of record." The total number of independents cannot be accurately reported, because no single agency or association collects such data. But the Independent Petroleum Association of America estimates that the total number of independent oil and

171

gas producers has dropped almost 50 percent to about eight thousand today from fifteen thousand in the early 1980s.

9. Quoted in "Vital Speeches of the Day," April 1, 1987, p. 384.

Chapter 2

1. *World Oil Trends*, 1991 edition, Cambridge Energy Research Associates and Arthur Andersen & Co., Cambridge, Mass., p. 44.
2. *Statistical Abstract of the United States*, 1991 edition, Tables 738, 739, p. 469.
3. *World Oil Trends*, op.cit.
4. In 1982, independent producers were responsible for 3,105 rotary rigs that employed 7,060 seismic crews drilling 7,386 wildcat wells. Four years later, the number of independently financed rotary rigs had dropped to 964, with seismic crews reduced to 2,355 and wildcat holes down to 3,484. The point: independents traditionally have been responsible for a high percentage of new discoveries. Once oil is found, the finder usually ties up with a major oil company, which has the necessary capital financing to develop and produce the well.
5. *Annual Energy Review*, 1991 edition, U.S. Department of Energy, Table 43.
6. *Rocky Mountain News*, September 26, 1992, p. 49.
7. According to the U.S. Department of Labor's Bureau of Labor Statistics, Texas oil and gas exploration employment fell to 164,800 in 1992 from 266,800 in 1982, Oklahoma dropped to 33,400 from 86,500, and Louisiana to 46,200 from 84,000.
8. *Statistical Abstract of the United States*, 1992 edition, Table 1003.9; *Statistical Abstract of the United States*, 1991 edition.
9. *Statistical Abstract of the United States*, 1991 edition.
10. A temporary sharp rise occurred during the Gulf War in early 1992, when the price leaped briefly above $30. But this was due to speculation among traders, not producers, that the war would severely restrict supplies. Within days, the price dipped back. The market realized that *all* production, not just oil inside the Arabian Gulf area, had to be taken into consideration when pricing spot-market oil.
11. *Herold's Annual Reserve Replacement Cost Analysis*, 25th edition (Greenwich, Ct: John S. Herold Inc.), p. 5.
12. According to the American Petroleum Institute's *Joint Association Survey of Drilling Costs*, the average drilling cost per foot for all new U.S. wells dropped from $77.02 per foot in 1980 to $76.07 by 1990. This indicates

that wildcatters were cutting their risk of losses by looking for shallow-depth oil in existing fields, not less proven, deeper zone areas where the odds of finding oil were not so good.

13. *Annual Energy Review*, 1991 Edition, Ibid., Tables 44, 53.
14. Arthur Andersen & Co. Oil and Gas Reserve Disclosures, 1985–89 Series, pp. 16–29.
15. *Annual Energy Review*, 1991 Edition, Table 42. These numbers should not suggest that there are no additional potential oil and gas reserves. To the contrary, there are good reasons for believing that major new finds are yet to be made, especially of natural gas.
16. A 1992 report by the research unit of the international investment company.
17. The *Energy Daily*, commentary by Charles DiBona, August 4, 1992.

CHAPTER 3

1. Independent Petroleum Association of America, 1991 annual report, p. 98.
2. *Natural Resources Tax Review*, September-October 1992, p. 475.
3. Ibid.
4. According to Cambridge Research, by 1990 this number had grown almost two full percentage points to 77 percent of the world's proven crude-oil reserves. OPEC member nations, in order of reserves (in billions of barrels of crude oil), are:

NATION	1990 PROVEN RESERVES
Saudi Arabia	257.6
Iraq	100.0
United Arab Emirates	98.1
Kuwait	97.1
Iran	92.9
Venezuela	58.5
Lybia	22.8
Nigeria	16.0
Algeria	9.2
Indonesia	8.2
Qatar	4.5
Ecuador	1.5
Gabon	0.7

Total OPEC reserves in 1990 were 767.1 billion barrels. In contrast, U.S. proven reserves totaled 25.9 billion barrels. The squeeze on domestic reserves is due to increased exploration by OPEC members (proven reserves grew almost 93 percent between 1970 and 1990) and declining activity in the U.S. (proven reserves fell by 13 percent, from 29.6 billion barrels in 1970).

5. James L. Dunlap, quoted in *Vital Speeches of the Day*, September-October, 1991, p. 73.
6. Burke, ibid, p. 479.

CHAPTER 4

1. Some "beautiful" wilderness areas in the Western U.S. "badlands" are at least as barren as land formerly stripped to mine coal. Beauty is, indeed, in the eye of the beholder. To the starving family, a lush moutainside astride unused coal is selfish negation of human development. And, conversely, the open-pit coal mine is exalted because its economic contribution enriches the lives of people and educates, feeds, and clothes children.
2. By way of comparison, the *Exxon Valdez* disaster in March 1989 released about 240,000 barrels of oil into Alaska's Prince William Sound, or more than three times the amount of crude oil discharged in the Santa Barbara spill.

CHAPTER 5

1. Daniel Yergin, *THE PRIZE: The Epic Quest for Oil, Money and Power* (New York, N.Y.: Simon & Schuster, 1991), p. 569.
2. Ibid., p. 571.
3. Ibid., p. 666.
4. Study by Gruy Engineering Corp. for the American Petroleum Institute.
5. Bureau of Land Managment, *Overview of the 1991 Arctic National Wildlife Refuge Recoverable Petroleum Reserve Data*, April 1991.
6. Robert D. Gunn, testifying before the U.S. House of Representatives Committee of Merchant Marine and Fisheries' Subcommittee on Fisheries and Wildlife Conservation and the Environment, Chairman Gerry E. Studds (D-Mass.), July 16, 1991.
7. According to Department of Energy Estimates, U.S. oil imports may

increase by more than 4 million barrels per day in the 1990s, increasing our oil dependence to more than 60 percent of our consumption at current rates.

8. Paul Rauber, *Sierra* magazine, Jan./Feb. 1992, p. 42.
9. "Potentially," because it has the possibility of containing 30 billion barrels of recoverable oil. If the more prudent 9.2 billion barrel estimates prevailed, the Arctic Wildlife Refuge would rank behind the Prudhoe Bay discovery.
10. Paul Rauber, *Sierra* magazine, Jan./Feb. 1992, p. 41.
11. Alaska Public Utilities Commission Annual Reports for 1993, 1991.

CHAPTER 6

1. Typically, when a 42-gallon barrel of crude oil is refined, about 46 percent of the product will be for vehicles and aviation gasoline, another 21 percent for home heating oil, and 11 percent for aviation jet fuel. The remainder, about 22 percent, is used in specialty manufacturing processes, such as chemicals and plastics, lubricants, petrochemical feedstocks, and so on. Source: the American Petroleum Institute.
2. Richard B. McKenzie, "Sense and Nonsense of Energy Conservation," *Society*, March 1992, p. 18.
3. Craig G. Goodman, vice president of governmental affairs for Mitchell Energy in Woodlands, Texas, and a former director of oil, economic, and energy tax policy for the U.S. Department of Energy; and Richard C. Gordon, senior director of the Petroleum Finance Co. of Washington, D.C., and former Phillips Petroleum Co. economist.
4. Statistical Abstract of the United States, 1991, Table 1330; U.S. Department of Commerce, unpublished data for 1992.
5. And this is only crude-oil imports. When you add all refined oil and other petroleum-related products, the 1990 value of imports totaled about $60.5 billion. Natural gas imports were relatively minor in comparison, or about $3.4 billion.
6. Don Hodel comments: "At the 1971 World Energy Conference in Bucharest, I became acutely aware of the singleness of Saudi Arabia's only asset: Oil. I returned and commented that it was foolish for us to expect the Saudis to keep increasing production from 10 to 15 to 20 million barrels per day just to satisfy the United States' seemingly insatiable appetite for oil. To do so would deplete their only 'cash crop,' and once it was gone they would have nothing left to sell. Then, with an attempt at humor, I

concluded by saying this would be true 'unless the sand and gravel business gets a whole lot better.' Sometime later, after a speech in which I made this remark, a man came forward and gently but authoritatively informed me that even that option was not open to the Saudis, because the sand was so smoothed from wind abrasion that it was unsuitable as a construction material, and sand for mixing concrete had to be imported."

7. See chapter 2 for a description of how dramatically rising energy costs affect the prices of all other consumer goods. If the 1970–80 era is any guide, a 5 percent increase in energy costs will produce a 1 percent rise in overall inflation, exclusive of the 5 percent jump in fuel expenses. This means that if, in a given year, oil and gas prices rose 20 percent—which has happened before—a typical consumer would pay 20 percent more for transportation and home-heating, and 4 percent more for all other commodities. The relationship is direct, and cannot be dismissed.

CHAPTER 7

1. *Christian Science Monitor*, September 3, 1992, p. 1.
2. Mexico restricts its oil exports to the United States to 50 percent or less of national production.
3. *New York Times* Sunday Magazine, March 7, 1993, p. 30.
4. *THE PRIZE*, New York, N.Y.: Simon & Schuster, 1991.
5. Quoted in *The Energy Daily*, September 4, 1992, p.1.

CHAPTER 8

1. They are Florida, Tennessee, Alabama, Arkansas, Georgia, New Mexico, Texas, Oklahoma, Arkansas, Indiana, Virginia, and Maryland.
2. These statistics were from the 1992 Statistical Abstract of the United States, as reported by the U.S. Department of Labor, the Census Bureau and Department of Commerce.
3. *Dallas Morning News*, April 26, 1993, pp. 1A, 12A-15A. It should be noted here that these figures were not reported in the context of a decline in the Texas oil and gas industry, but in a series of articles comparing the quality of life in California compared with Texas. Even so, the statistical data relating to Texas clearly reveal a growth of social problems that can be attributed, at least in part and probably mostly, to the decline in family incomes and tax-supported social services that occurred when the Texas oil patch became impoverished.

CHAPTER 9

1. Not every alternative energy source displaces oil, of course. Some of these substitutes replace coal, nuclear fuels, hydroelectric power, and so on. But others do replace oil. Among these are ethanol and methanol fuels, natural gas vehicles, and electricity from generating plants that are capable of economically converting from oil fuels to other sources (although these are relatively few in number).
2. American Petroleum Institute databank.
3. *American Energy Review 1991*, Energy Information Institute, U.S. Department of Energy, Washington, D.C., p. 93, Table 41.
4. Reuters Financial Report, June 29, 1993. Speech of Dr. Subroto to the National Energy Summit sponsored by the Jefferson Energy Foundation.
5. At the end of 1991, the Strategic Petroleum Reserve held the equivalent of 86 days of net oil imports. *Annual Energy Review 1991*, op. cit., p. 95, Table 42.
6. In contrast, the rig count in the Middle East rose to 162 in March 1993 from 149 in March 1992—Middle Eastern fields are so rich that fewer rigs are required to find and produce oil—and rose even more in Canada, to 237 rigs in March 1993 from only eighty-six the prior year, more proof of how foreign oil producers are thriving at the expense of domestic U.S. operators.
7. See chapter 3, Robert Gunn estimate.
8. Energy Information Administration, U.S. Department of Energy. This was a verbal estimate provided in 1993.

INDEX

179

Btu tax, 147–150, 152
Bureau of Labor Statistics, oil and gas
    industry employment, 23–24, 172n
Bureau of Land Management, 63, 79
Burke, Frank M., Jr., 45
Bush, George
    economic reason for defeat, 126
    foreign imports, 13
Byrd, Sen. Robert, 147

C

CAFE standards. *See* Corporate average
    fuel efficiency standards
California
    job potential from development of
        Alaskan oil fields, 82, 83
    off-shore drilling ban, 60–62
    Santa Barbara oil leak, 59–60, 73, 74
Carbon tax, 147–148, 150
Caribou
    feeding patterns, 80
    herd size, 164
    migration patterns, 74
Carter, Jimmy, speed limit lowering, 29
Cement industry, 26
Center for Strategic and International
    Studies, 115
Chevron
    Arctic National Wildlife Refuge
        development, 86
    Fortune magazine assessment of
        prospects, 9
Clean Air Act of 1967, 59, 73
Clinton administration
    aid to former Soviet Union, 114–
        115
    efforts to reduce demand for oil, 97
    energy taxes, 110, 114, 118, 147–
        150, 152
Coalition for American Energy Security,
    116

Colorado, family income decline, 132
Consumer Price Index
    energy costs, 22–23
    rate of inflation, 16
Cook Inlet, Alaska, 169
Coors Energy Co., 62–64, 68
Core inflation, 8
Corporate average fuel efficiency
    standards, 28–29
CPI. *See* Consumer Price Index

D

Depletion allowance, 37, 39, 43–45,
    162–163
Derr, Ken, 11
Desert Shield, 68, 102
Desert Storm, 68, 102, 119
DiBona, Charles, 13, 33–34
Discovery of oil, 5–7
Drilling mud
    Alaska pipeline and, 77–78
    hazardous waste classification, 66–67,
        165–166
Dunlap, James L., 47

E

Earth First, 85, 86, 88
Electricity, 142
Employment issues
    Arctic National Wildlife Refuge job
        potential, 81–84
    collateral employment, 25–26
    domestic employment, 10–11, 12,
        16
    oil price impact, 22–26
    rig count and, 27–28, 177n
    unemployment costs, 132–134
Energy taxes, 41–42, 110, 114, 118,
    147–150, 152

ABOUT THE AUTHORS

Donald Paul Hodel served successively as Under Secretary of the Interior, Secretary of Energy, and Secretary of the Interior in the administration of President Ronald Reagan. He is a former Administrator of the Bonneville Power Administration and is currently principal of Summit Group International, a consulting firm in the energy and natural resources fields, and director on a number of boards. He lives with his wife, Barbara, in Silverthorne, Colorado.

Robert Deitz has been a reporter, editor, and author since 1962, most recently as executive business editor and columnist for the late *Dallas Times Herald*. He was a 1971–72 Nieman Fellow in Journalism at Harvard University, and is coauthor of books on the savings and loan industry (1989) and the Rodney King trial (1992). In addition to books, he writes a syndicated business column and, with his wife, Sharon, lives in Dallas.